THE PLAGUE

NOTES

including
- *Life of Camus*
- *Camus and the Absurd*
- *List of Characters*
- *Critical Commentaries*
- *Character Analyses*
- *Allegory*
- *Review Questions and Theme Topics*
- *Selected Bibliography*

by
Gary Carey, M.A.
University of Colorado

Cliffs Notes

INCORPORATED

LINCOLN, NEBRASKA 68501

Editor

Gary Carey, M.A.
University of Colorado

Consulting Editor

James L. Roberts, Ph.D.
Department of English
University of Nebraska

Cliffs Notes, Inc.   Lincoln, Nebraska

CONTENTS

The Plague

LIFE OF CAMUS

Albert Camus was born November 7, 1913, and reared in Algeria, a country exposed to the blistering African sun and the plain of the Mediterranean sea. These roots—the sun and the sea—have spread into all of Camus' writings—the novels, the plays, and the essays. They are a part of his lyricism, his symbolism, and his values. The universe, it seems from his early *Noces,* was mother, father, and lover for the young Camus, and from the first, Camus was aware of the paradoxical aspects of his natural world. The sensual free pleasure of swimming and hiking was in continuous contrast to the bare stony earth that made living a matter of poverty and destitution. He was early aware of the absurd condition of man's being totally alone in a resplendent universe. This concept is Camus' equivalent "In the beginning. . . ." Against its truth, all of his writings sound revolt, for he refused to be deceived by social religions or individual submissions that ignored or defied the irreducible truth that man alone is responsible for himself, his meaning, and his measure. Camus' writings are a testament to a continuing belief in man's exiled but noble condition.

Lucien Camus, Albert's father, was killed in 1914 during World War I's Battle of the Marne and the year-old child was reared by his deaf mother. She had little money and was apparently a rather joyless and boring companion for her son. It is little wonder that he spent much of his time with athletics, studies, and necessary part-time employment. When he finished school, a university degree seemed the most important challenge available to a poverty-stricken student. Like Dr. Rieux, the narrator of *The Plague,* he was enthusiastic about studies and was ambitious. He was not able to complete his studies immediately, however. In 1930, while he was a student of philosophy at the University of Algiers, Camus almost died during a first long bout with tuberculosis, an illness which would periodically afflict him for many years. Then, after his recovery, he was beset by the constant problem of poverty and was forced to support himself for several years as variously a meteorologist, a police clerk, and a salesman. During this time he married and divorced and also joined and left the Communist party. In 1935, a year before he received his degree from the University, he founded The Workers' Theater, a group formed to present plays for Algiers' working population. Before his theater venture ended in 1939, Camus had published *L'Envers et L'Endroit (Betwixt and Between),* essays that deal with man and death in terms of his oblivious universe. They are mood pieces, written in his own mixture of irony and lyricism, describing man's defenselessness and his isolation in a splendid universe whose only rule for man seems to be death. There is an early optimism in these essays; it is here that Camus first advocates living as if man had eternal value. He believes that only in man's courageous rebellion to confront himself and his world can he begin to create a civilization that can rescue itself from a nihilistic catastrophe.

Between the years 1937 and 1939 Camus wrote book reviews and occasional essays for the *Alger-Republicain,* a left wing newspaper. Later he assumed the editorship of the *Soir-Republicain,* but for only a short time. He was severely critical of the French colonial government and after the newspaper folded, soon found himself unofficially unwelcome and unable to find a job in the country. Thus in 1940 he left Algeria and went to live in Paris. There he worked for a time with the *Paris-Soir,* but his journalistic career was once again curtailed. This time the Germans had invaded France. Much like the character Rambert in *The Plague,* Camus left the battlefield. He returned once again to North Africa, where he remarried and began teaching in a private school in Oran. He continued to write and by now had filled several notebooks with sketches and several versions of *The Stranger* and *The Myth of Sisyphus.* He also worked on background ideas for a new novel, *The Plague.*

A year later, both *The Stranger* and *Myth* were published and Camus was established as a writer of international importance. *The Stranger's* Meursault has since become a literary archetype, and the beginning sentences of *The Stranger* have become synonymous with an absurd or ironic situation. Never before had the public read about a man who was so absolutely honest as Meursault. In fact, his honesty is perhaps his only meritorious quality. Meursault is an anti-hero, an inconspicuous clerk who does not believe in God, but cannot lie. He does believe in going to the movies, swimming, and making love. He is finally beheaded because he murdered an Arab; he is condemned, however, because he seemed indifferent at his mother's funeral. Meursault becomes aware of his freedom and his happiness only after he is imprisoned, a situation similar to that of the imprisoned Oranian citizens in *The Plague.* He faces death with sensitive and joyous awareness of his last moments and hopes for a vivid end and an angry shouting crowd as witness.

In the year of *The Stranger,* 1941, Camus decided to return to France and commit himself to the French Resistance Movement. He enlisted in an organization known as "Combat," also the title of the clandestine newspaper he edited during the Occupation. After Paris was liberated in 1944,

Camus continued to edit *Combat* for four years while he published collections of his wartime essays. His plays *The Misunderstanding* and *Caligula* were presented during 1944; the latter was as well received as the former was not. In 1945, Camus toured the United States, lecturing and gathering firsthand impressions of the national power that was credited with ending the long war.

His allegory, *The Plague,* was published in June, 1947, and was immediately cited as a major literary work. The critics and the public were unanimous in their praise for this somberly narrated chronicle. As a popular book it had none of the formula gimmicks; it had no great love plot-line, no fascinating setting, or even powerfully drawn characterizations. But to a nation recovering from an enemy occupation, it was an authentic account of months during which only human dignity and survival mattered. Postwar readers were appreciative and sympathetic to this writer who had faithfully, and not melodramatically, recorded the suffering and misery of separation and exile.

In 1949, upon his return to France from a South American tour, Camus became quite ill and went into almost total seclusion, only occasionally publishing collections of more of his political essays. In 1951, when he was recovered, he published an extensive study of metaphysical, historical, and artistic revolt, *The Rebel.* It was an extremely controversial book and was responsible for breaking the friendship between Camus and Jean Paul Sartre.

After *The Rebel,* Camus began translating favorite works of international playwrights. His adaptations were rapidly produced and included Calderón's *La Devocion de la Cruz,* Larivey's *Les Espirits,* Buzzati's *Un Caso Clinico,* Faulkner's *Requiem for a Nun,* and others. More collections of his political essays appeared, plus many prefaces to contemporary writings.

In 1956 a new fictional work appeared, his novel *The Fall.* Unlike the technique of his other two novels, the narrative is not in the third person but in the first person, and the story does not take place in North Africa, but in Amsterdam. The book deals with a successful and admired lawyer who suddenly faces his conscience after he refuses to help a woman drowning in a suicide attempt. The confessions of his fraud and guilt contain precise and penetrating comments about contemporary society. It is not as ambitious or as lengthy as *The Plague,* but it is as polished a masterpiece as *The Stranger.*

The following year Camus was awarded the Nobel Prize for Literature and two years later he was dead, killed in an automobile accident on January 4, 1960. The many eulogistic essays which appeared afterward remarked on the absurdity of his death – its suddenness, its uselessness, and the lack of logic to explain why. Camus, however, was probably more aware of the significance of his individual life than any of his essayists; his meaningless death is the key witness to his body of literature.

CAMUS AND THE ABSURD

To enter into the literary world of Albert Camus, one must realize, first off, that one is dealing with an author who does not believe in God. Major characters in Camus' fiction, therefore, can probably be expected either to disbelieve or to wrestle with the problem of belief. One's first response then, as a reader, might profitably be a brief consideration of what might happen to a character who comes to realize that there is no Divinity, no God. What happens when he realizes that his death is final, that his joys, his disappointments, and his sufferings are brief flickers preluding an afterlife of nothingness? What changes in his daily pattern of work-eat-love-sleep must he now effect? Much like Kafka's Joseph K., the man in question has staggeringly comprehended that he is condemned to an eternal void – and because of no crime. Only because he is a part of a meaningless birth-death cycle is he doomed; the fact of death and his mortality is all. He sees, in short, The End focused on the screen of his future, the screen on which he used to project his dreams and hopes. Hope based on anything superhuman is now futile. He sees an end for him and for his fellowmen. So, what then? Suicide, if all is meaningless? Or a blind return flight toward an external, though ever-silent, God?

This concern with death and its abyss of nonexistence is the basis for most of Camus' literary works. Condemned to an everlasting zero of eternity, Camus' characters often suffer their author's own involvement and anguish; and, for his readers, the recognition of the fact of their own deaths is the starting point for their confronting and experiencing Camus' concept of the Absurd.

As a salvation, however, from despair and nihilism, Camus' Absurd embraces a kind of positive optimism – optimism in the sense that much emphasis is placed on human responsibility for civilizing the world. The fictional characters, therefore, who shoulder their new *mortal* responsibility, are often characterized as rebels. In revolt from both a cowardly suicide and an equally cowardly faith flight, the new optimism suggests man's returning to the center of a philosophical tightrope above an intensely physical death and, in his revolt, performing precariously. Above the threat of death, in confrontation with death, the metaphysical ropewalker acts "as if" his actions mattered. Obviously they don't in any long-range sense. And, rather than scamper to either the poles of Hope or Suicide, he knows that he will eventually fall, but stays mid-center. Obviously his life, the lives of all men do not *finally* matter. Death is definitive. But, clown-like, he creates new acts, new entertainments — reaching, gesturing. Exploiting his precarious posture in a new burst of freedom, he restructures his actions, and in vivid contrast to death, he diffuses joy and a sense of ridiculous responsibility.

Walking on this razor's edge of "as if" means that man must act to his fellowmen as though life had meaning; in short, living an absurdity. Knowing that man has only man to depend upon, however, he can take fresh courage. He is now rid of fearful superstitions and questioning theories; he can now discard the religious faiths which assume man is subservient to a Something divine and eternal. Man now has no excuse for failure, save himself. "God's Will" as a pocket excuse for failure is no longer valid. Man succeeds or fails because of the strength, or the lack of it, in himself. Each man is acting as a representative of all mankind; he is responsible for creating peace in the world. No longer will Sunday's prayers excuse Saturday's hates. He is responsible for all and is totally alone. Camus challenges man to do the work which he has hitherto assigned to God.

LIST OF CHARACTERS

Dr. Bernard Rieux
The surgeon-narrator of *The Plague*.

Jean Tarrou
The best friend of Rieux. His notebooks are used as part of the chronicle.

Father Paneloux
A priest in Oran.

Raymond Rambert
A Paris journalist trapped in Oran.

Joseph Grand
   A petty official, also a writer.

Cottard
   A criminal who hides from arrest in Oran.

M. Michel
   A concierge, the plague's first victim.

Madame Rieux
   The mother of Dr. Rieux. She comes to visit her son during the first days of the plague.

Madame Rieux
   Dr. Rieux' wife, who dies in a mountain sanitarium outside Oran.

The old Spaniard
   An asthmatic philosopher.

M. Othon
   Oran's police magistrate.

Jacques Othon
   A young victim of the plague, son of the police magistrate.

Dr. Richard
   A conservative colleague of Dr. Rieux.

Prefect
   The chief magistrate of Oran.

Dr. Castel
   An elderly doctor who perfects a new plague serum.

Jeanne Grand
   The divorced wife of the petty official.

Gonzales, Garcia, Raoul, Marcel, and Louis
   Rambert's underground contacts.

CRITICAL COMMENTARIES

PART ONE

The tragedy of a plague is announced in the book's title. It is also underscored in the first chapter. This technique, it is worth noting, is somewhat similar to that of a Greek tragedy. Here also we know in advance the horrible fate in store for the characters, and we watch as the scenes unfold the familiar fate and the agony of, say, Oedipus or Creon.

While reading this novel, one should remember that Camus has an initial prerequisite for an understanding of his philosophy of the absurd: a realization and a recognition of the fact of one's own death. A man only begins living, according to Camus, when he announces in advance his own death to himself and realizes the consequences. This is, in a sense, what Camus is doing in the opening scenes of *The Plague*. He is announcing the deaths of many people, common people, and as spectators, we will wait, watch, hear, and perhaps learn from the consequences of the everyday Oedipuses and Creons of Oran—citizens warned again and again of their fate to die, yet who choose to be unbelieving, antagonistic, and indifferent to the warning. The announcement of death is paramount in Camus' philosophy and in his novels.

In the first paragraph of the book, the ordinariness of Oran is contrasted with the extraordinary business of the plague, and on the surface the comment seems possibly only a bit of literary formula. Camus, however, had good reason for beginning his work with just such a contrast. In his volume of essays, *The Myth of Sisyphus*, published five years before *The Plague,* he says that contrasts between the natural and the extraordinary, the individual and the universal, the tragic and the everyday are essential ingredients for the absurd work. Camus conceived of the universe in terms of paradoxes and contrasts: man lives, yet he is condemned to die; most men live within the context of an afterlife, yet there has never been proof that an afterlife exists. Camus' idea of living meaningfully, yet knowing full well that life has no eventual meaning, is a positive-negative contrast. It is natural, then, for him to begin and set his novel in terms of an extreme contrast.

Still considering his setting, note that Camus has done two things with Oran as a stage for his chronicle. As an actual Algerian town in North Africa, it functions as an anchor of reality for the reader. The book, after all, is an allegory, but becomes more successful in all its levels partly because of its existent geographic setting. *Gulliver's Travels* has improbable place names, as does *Erewhon,* and both works have a fairy tale quality, largely because of their ambiguous settings. *The Plague,* on the other hand, is more satisfying on the literal level because of its specifically placed setting, and, in addition, the literal level has more concern for the human condition than, say, the literal level of *Gulliver's Travels.*

Camus was not, however, to faithfully render Oran much further than geographically locating it for the reader. Once he set the novel in the hot, arid region of North Africa and had captured our belief in its existence, he began recreating Oran and its people in Western terms. Oran is not the typical Mediterranean town described in guidebooks as having a "delightfully sunny complexion and charming little balconies overhanging narrow streets, with delightful glimpses of shady courtyards." Camus refutes this armchair attitude; he characterizes the town as filled with bored people, people who have cultivated habits, people whose chief interest is "doing business." This is far from the romantic Mediterranean town we might expect on the shores of the sea. These people Camus describes are recognizable as Americans and as western Europeans. There are numerous articles written in popular magazines satirizing our culture as mechanistic and materialistic. And, in his quiet way, Camus is also using satire. He is showing people who choose to spend their time commercially, people who "fritter away" what time is left for living. He has, then, created a city far enough away esthetically and geographically for his artistic purposes, but one which has the tempo and coloring of our own environment.

Examining the city more closely, the narrator says that love is particularly repulsive in Oran. People either have intercourse much as robots might, or they go about it animal-like—all this, he says because they lack time and thinking. Camus has often been characterized as a godless Christian, meaning that he expounds all the Christian virtues, but only in terms of man. Love, for Camus, is a mixture of "desire, affection, and intelligence." It is given to other men instead of to God. In this sense, man is sacred, but absurdly sacred; he may die in any moment, just as love may disappear within a moment. Yet one must live committed "as if" man and love ultimately mattered. The concern with love gone wrong is a symptom of an illness within Oran even before the plague of death strikes.

Having briefly illuminated Oran's life and love, the next focus is naturally enough on the other end of the human cycle—death. Death is a "discomfort." The tone here is low-keyed because the narrator is speaking of the normal day-to-day process of dying. And if fatality is wretched normally, imagine what discomfort will be encountered during the pages of this long chronicle of death. The casual mention here is being heavily underplayed.

Even now, perhaps, one believes that the novel will not be so wholly concerned with death, but it will be. Here is a point, brief as it is, of normalcy to weigh later against the extreme. The mention of a "normal" dying man, "trapped behind hundreds of walls all sizzling with heat," suggests the mazes of Dante's hell, mazes which must be traversed before the plague's thousands of deaths are tolled. And since Camus has lamented that man's imagination has ceased to function, perhaps the reader would do well to expand it here in this trapped, sizzling, "normal" situation of death and imagine the eventual effect of the plague.

The emphasis on the habits which have been formed and cultivated by the "soulless" people of Oran are significant. Vital living can be stifled by habits: in Oran, love-making is relegated to the weekends. Camus has said in one of his essays that the absurd is often encountered when one is suddenly aware that habits have strangled natural responses and reactions, that habits have simplified one into simplemindedness. It is at this point that one should revolt against his stultifying pattern of living. Recognition of bottomless death makes a habit-bound life even more absurd. Camus seems, then, to be creating a society of habit-oriented people in order to confront them with death in its most horrible form—the plague. Then, from this confrontation, new values regarding living will emerge.

"It is impossible to see the sea," the narrator tells us. Oran turns its back on the bay. The sea, of course, is a striking symbol for life, richly and lushly lived. Camus himself loved the sea; when he swam in it, he encountered it nakedly and boldly, in a way virtually impossible to encounter society. Societies too often contain hypocrisy and jealousy; there is seldom honesty and directness. One knows what he encounters when he swims. In social waters, swimming is done blindly. Oran turns its back on nature, on sincerity, and truth; its concern is with the materialistic and the habitual. As a natural and symbolic backdrop the sea, with its unbound waves, is an ever-present, ominous comment on the action.

The narrator's insistence on the book's objectivity stresses his wish to present the truth, as nearly as possible. He lists his data and where he got them. He will tell, he says, "what happened." Knowing, of course, that he (the narrator) is Dr. Rieux, we can see a kind of scientific detachment to his style, in addition to his hope to be objectively truthful.

The style, which is semi-documentary, is reminiscent of journalism. Perhaps Camus' several years of newspaper writing were the genesis of this style or helped formulate his ideas concerning the need for careful, documented truthfulness. In any case, the reader should note that Camus does not single out lovers clinging together during a plague situation to snare his readers' attention. He hopes to tell his story authentically, directing the narrative to our intellect and our imagination rather than to our heart strings. His result has the tone of precision — much the same as Truman Capote's nonfiction novel *In Cold Blood.*

The reader should also remember that the book is not, per se, a novel; the volume is a chronicle, and thus we should not expect avant garde or impressionistic devices — nothing except, as nearly as possible, a factual account of a plague and the people affected.

In addition, Camus is striving for an esthetic distance between the reader and the novel which will keep the reader an observer. Close identification, a major objective for most fiction authors, is to be avoided because emotional involvement will keep us from seeing the book as, at least, a three-dimensional allegory. Camus' immediately attacking the problem of exposition and setting, and defining them simply and directly, establishes a tone which he will hold until the book's end. This objective tone is particularly important because by underplaying the sensationalism of the plague, he hopes to startle our intellect more completely to its lessons. In this first chapter, then, he has rather formally given us the setting, almost dryly discoursed on its features, and finished his brief, journalistically sounding framework for the action to follow.

The chronicle's action, however, develops slowly. *The Plague's* first chapter is a rather neat, concise package of setting and background, and Chapter 2 is, in a sense, another such block of writing, somewhat like a second solid step taken into the novel, but with a difference. Chapter 1 is written in a sum-up style by a narrator who slips us occasional asides throughout his short discourse. This narrator slips out of Chapter 2 and the book moves forward with conventional plot interest and the introduction of several main characters, yet it retains Chapter 1's sense of structural completeness. The chapter begins with Dr. Rieux's discovering a dead rat and a crotchety concierge's indignant and comic fussings and it ends with a total of several thousands of dead rats, plus the plague's first death — M. Michel, the concierge. The first dead rat begins the chapter; the first victim ends it.

Some of Camus' descriptions of the rats in this chapter are worth brief notice. The townspeople of Oran insist that the rats are surely meaningless, whereas the rats are extremely meaningful. Black is white to the people, and Camus' adjectives, in a parallel, often describe something quite the opposite of what is. For example, Dr. Rieux feels something "soft" under his foot. Usually *soft* is associated only with pleasant sensations, but here it is used in reverse. It describes the bloated corpse of a rat. Shortly thereafter, when a rat comes from the sewer it is described as spinning on itself with a little squeal, a sort of miniature ballet before death. In fact, Camus says later that the rats were coming out in long swaying lines and doing "a sort of pirouette." He describes the blood puddles around their noses as looking like red flowers. Again, as in Chapter 1, he uses an extreme contrast — here, to point to the absurdity of the symptoms: rats can't be seeping out of houses and sewers for a reason — rats' deaths can't be beautiful. Yet both are.

This is a small point, for there is much description of the rats as repulsive and rotting, but Camus' occasional contrasts of appearance versus reality in his description is exactly what the chapter is concerned with.

The character focus of the book is not wholly on Dr. Rieux, but because he is, in disguise, the narrator, he assumes a kind of early main-character or hero focal point. Studying his reaction to the dead rats — the symptoms of the plague — we find him to be a common-sense type of "hero." Camus does not slide him into a pivotal part to be an obvious mouthpiece for any heroics of philosophizing or, for that matter, any other kind of typical heroics. Rieux is a doctor; throughout the book, he doctors.

As a character, he is initially fleshed out with a good deal of personal preoccupation when he first encounters the dead rats. The blood leaking from their mouths reminds him of his wife's illness and her imminent trip to a mountain sanatorium. Their numbers seem only an oddity, a curiosity. He shrugs away the matter, saying "it'll pass." It is, however, Rieux's early indifference to the rats which eventually passes. With his wife away, he is left in a perspective larger than any plagued romantic tragedy. He is totally pledged to the populace, but not even yet does he divine what it is that hovers over Oran. Plague never enters his head. When the garbage cans begin filling with rats, he telephones the sanitation department — a businesslike and correct way to deal with the situation. Indeed, this thorough and methodical attitude will continue throughout his dealings with the plague. His is a quiet, unsensational role, but it is exemplary in that he is totally committed to his fellow men and has "no truck with injustice or compromises with the truth."

Another character, although her part in the book is small, is introduced in this first chapter and is important because she exhibits a general Oranian attitude toward the plague's symptoms. "It's like that sometimes," says Rieux's mother, suggesting a seen-much, lived-through-much mind. She survives. She has seen depression, a loss of her husband, has surely even seen war; besides, she's with her son. She'll decide the importance of this unpleasant talk about rats when need be.

Jean Tarrou, on the other hand, is intrigued. This is a wholly new experience and he savors it.

Very briefly, we also meet in this chapter the senile, chuckling old Spaniard. Perhaps because he is so near death himself, he enjoys with relish the instinctive feeling that he will not die alone but with numerous companions.

The journalist Rambert seems, at this point, only a foil for Rieux. His role will enlarge as the story develops. At present, he admits that he works for a newspaper that compromises with truth. Rieux, of course, is intolerant of such a situation and abruptly ends their conversation.

Grand, too, seems to furnish a foil-like situation for a deeper insight into Rieux's character. Being poor, Grand is not charged for the doctor's visits. Rieux responds immediately to the old man's call for help—help for a neighbor who has tried to hang himself. Further, he says he will ask, as a favor for the man, that the police inspector hold up the inquiry for a couple of days. When Grand explains "one's got to help a neighbor, hasn't one?" the doctor's several instances of demonstrated humanity are now even more clearly emphasized.

Richard, the telephoned colleague of Dr. Rieux, exhibits an oft-used approach of intellectuals toward problems. The situation of the rats may or may not be considered "normal," he says. His defense is with a semantic shield.

In the beginning, then, the rats are a ready topic of conversation for the townspeople, drawing them together in chattery groups. Later the Oranians become vaguely uneasy. The rats, they say, are disgusting, obnoxious, and a nuisance. When a total of some 8,000 dead rats is made public, there is even a demand for some kind of action and an accusation of carelessness is made against the sanitation bureau. But, when the symptoms suddenly vanish—tritely, like the sudden calm before a storm—all concern vanishes and the people breathe, as Camus says ironically, more freely.

Considering now Chapter 3, we find yet another kind of "package" chapter than either 1 or 2. So that the book will not have a one-viewpoint narrative, the author of the chronicle offers the notebooks of—not an

Oranian—but those of an outsider, Jean Tarrou. By presenting another viewpoint, that of someone who has no family or loved ones affected by the plague to color his account in his notebooks, the truth of "what happened" will be more nearly correct. Of course, Rieux, the doctor-narrator is, as nearly as possible, scientifically objective in his reporting, but the account of Tarrou aids and insures even greater honesty in the finished statement concerning this period. It is Tarrou who will supply the details to fill in the broader narrative outlines of Rieux. These details are the gears and wheels of Rieux's project of truth; they are the bits of conversation, street-corner portraits, the city's nerve ends.

Where Tarrou has come from is a mystery, but after several days of minute observation of the city, he writes: "At last!" Thus, it seems as though he is searching for an endpoint or goal of some sort—and has found it in Oran. But what interests him most about Oran? Surprisingly, it is the town's ugliness, its lack of trees, its hideous houses, and the ridiculous layout. He takes particular delight in regularly watching an old man coax cats beneath his balcony then, ecstatically, spitting on them. Tarrou's mention of the old man's finally spitting into space one day when the cats fail to appear is another voice to convince and remind us of what Rieux has said earlier about the town. It is bound, perhaps even strangling itself, with habits.

The mercantile air of Oran also pleases Tarrou. Perhaps he is looking for an epitomy of modern foulness. If so, this amplifies the narrator's comment in Chapter 2 comparing the rats to pus, oozing from the abscesses beneath the town.

There is more, though, to Tarrou than a seemingly morbid curiosity. Rieux notes his sense of humor, his love of swimming, and his fondness for the company of dancers and musicians. More important, he is a questioner and a self-examiner. He wonders about wasting time, for example, and his present answer is "by being fully aware of it," one does not waste it. As a reader, you might consider how he would view the old Spaniard who carefully puts dried peas from one pot to another. Is the old man aware of what he is doing? Is he wasting time?

This idea of not wasting time and of infusing the utmost consciousness into the present moment is an important existential tenet. This minute— *now*—this is what matters. Tarrou's suggestion that one might profitably remain on a balcony during a Sunday afternoon is reminiscent of what Meursault of Camus' *The Stranger* does on Sunday afternoon—watching, looking, seeing. All of this can be an exercise, if done consciously, to revolt against time's silent, sure murder of the body.

Tarrou says he is only interested in acquiring peace of mind. Why, then, would he come to Oran? This is a question to speculate about after we know Tarrou more thoroughly. For the present, he records the snatches of shallow gossip in Oran: the decay of the rats' bodies is seen as the only danger. That the rats themselves mean something more serious is ignored by the general population.

Only once in his notebooks does Tarrou add a comment after his scraps of reportage. He speculates on a musician who continues to play his trombone after he knows that his lungs are dangerously weak. Why Tarrou singles out this particular instance to comment on is fairly obvious. Tarrou, besides liking musicians, sees Oran as a town built of physical ugliness and of a sterile commercial spirit. Here is a man who challenges death in this repulsive setting and accomplishes what he desires most — making music. He is somewhat of an oddity in Tarrou's album of sketches.

Rieux includes a brief physical description of himself written by Tarrou, and then ends the chapter which seems, on the whole, somewhat fragmentary. Like Meursault, Tarrou is unconcerned about most things. He seems disconnected, interested primarily in himself. But because he shows little concern for the rats, but is sufficiently fascinated by Oran to record its idiosyncrasies, he is excellent for Rieux's purpose — a substantiation in presenting as accurate a picture as possible about the first days of the plague.

As the plague gently begins its slaughter, Dr. Rieux discovers in Chapter 4 that he must battle another plague-like phenomenon — the so-called red tape of bureaucracy. The frustration is Kafkaesque. Rieux is also convinced that the victims of the unidentified fever should be put in isolation, yet he is stopped because of his colleagues' insistence that there is no definite proof that the disease is dangerously infectious. The other doctors refuse to draw conclusions or make an attempt to consider the cases. Rieux is futilely attempting a professional search for the truth. The atmosphere is as oppressive as a sickroom. Like the sudden relief from the rats before the plague sets in, the patients all seem to take a turn for the better just before their death struggles. The reality is like a bad dream — absurd. There is a breakdown in communication between Rieux and other men. Rieux seems isolated — in miniature, a situation akin to the total isolation which the plague will eventually impose upon Oran.

This isolation of Rieux and of Oran is buttressed by one of Camus' exacting images. Referring once more to Oran's position on the sea, he says that it is humped "snail-wise" on the plateau. The image expands and colors the chapter. A snail's pace is exactly the tempo that the town has taken concerning the investigation of the curious fever deaths. And a snail's shell of indifference and ignorance is hiding the townspeople and even Rieux's colleagues from the truth. Even before the crises that the plague will create, here is a crisis of major importance – a crisis for truth.

This chapter also provides a fuller treatment of the character of Grand. Earlier, he has said "one's got to help a neighbor, hasn't one?" and suggested a Samaritan attitude. This impression is now modified. He did not discover Cottard as a result of his coming for a friendly visit. He read the shocking chalk-scrawled note on Cottard's door and dashed in. Talking about Cottard, Grand says that the only previous instance of any odd behavior is that the fellow always seemed to want to start a conversation. Why didn't Grand respond then?

Grand seems paradoxical. He is sure that he is a good neighbor, but is he? On the contrary, he appears to be much more concerned with words than he does with people. His dictionaries, his blackboard, the crammed-full portfolio, his study of Latin to perfect his French – all this – his search for the basic, the Ur-origins – is admirable, but he seems, thus far, neglecting the people who speak the language he delves into. Consider, too, the fact that Grand has a "finical anxiety" about his speech. But what comes out of his mouth? Empty phrases that he gropes forward with – phrases like "his grim resolve" and "his secret grief," phrases that border on being clichés. Language is living. His search is for a knowledge that will produce a perfect prose. Again, this is a marvelous sort of endeavor, but the result will be too perfect. It will be artificial and devoid of that vital flush of life that separates an artist from a craftsman.

Leaving Grand, Rieux tends more patients. The swollen ganglia which he sees recurring are often lanced and disgorge a mixture of blood and pus. This idea of disgorging is similar to the disgorging of the bloodied, bloated rats from beneath the town – another parallel image-idea of Camus'.

And Camus proves as facile with the paradoxical. The rats were headlines in the press. The ganglia deaths are not even mentioned, and a certain knowing cynicism about journalists' reporting only what happens in the streets – not behind closed doors – reveals Camus' ever serious concern with truth.

The chapter ends with Rieux hesitating before he actually acknowledges, pronouncing the words, that this is indeed plague which is beginning to devour Oran. An older doctor is present and urges him to admit it. As he does, Rieux is staring at the cliffs, the piece of bay, the sky—at nature, at creativity; he says "plague" to himself, and his thoughts of impending death create a polar contrast with the free, natural scene before him.

Rieux's initial acceptance of the plague is a major scene in this first section, and as relief from this tension Chapter 5 briefly changes the pace. This chapter is a kind of didactic catch-all for Camus-Rieux to vent personal feelings about the plague and all its implications.

Here again we see Rieux as quite the opposite of a wily Odysseus hero-type or an undaunted chivalric figure. He is staggered by the knowledge that he has reasoned out for himself. And, if up to now he has been one step ahead of the townspeople in conscientiously trying to isolate and arrest this mysterious virus, he has never completely stopped and considered the panorama of torment which will be in store for the prey of the plague. Rieux, as narrator, castigates the townspeople for their stupidity and frivolity, these people who refuse to conjure and consider consequences. He sees them as pitiful, and universal, dupes of illusion.

The plague is an enigma to the doctor. Its death-dealing powers are so enormous that his imagination fails to respond to the figure of a hundred million deaths, a figure he reckons as the historical toll of plague.

All imaginations cope ineffectually with such a figure, but the doctor's problem is compounded by the fact that he deals daily in death and has seen the raw damage that statistics are charted from. It should be especially noted here that the doctor is attempting an emotional response to the advent of plague. His try at imagining the annihilation of five movie houses of people is an attempt to arrive at something concrete and meaningful. His thoughts of fellow Athenians fighting one another centuries ago for burial rite space for their dead foreshadows a like battle he will fight when he attempts to properly care for the sick and dying.

In contrast to his quandary in this chapter, the natural beauty of the outside beams healthily. As he watches and listens, it is the sea he hears most clearly as it murmurs with unrest, affirming "the precariousness of all things in this world." His coming-to-terms with whatever has invaded Oran must be accomplished soon, but with reason and observation. He does not undergo here a metamorphosis and emerge something much grander than before. His determination to be simply efficient and thorough is his answer for the present—doing one's job as it should be done. This is the careful, exact quality in Rieux that we have seen previously. He has considered, speculated, yet returned to his familiar role of the dedicated, common-sense doctor.

This speculation of Rieux's turns into musings throughout Chapter 6. He muses on the dimensions of Grand's character—measurements which are unexceptional, but important in their implications. Two things are done here with Grand. His unimportance is particularized and then this non-importance is generalized into symbolic significance.

First, Rieux considers Grand's occupation as clerk. He seems to manage, cheerfully enough, on what certainly can't be more than a pittance of a salary. The reader must here see Grand against the background described earlier. Most of Oran talks, scribbles, and muscles their days into ample financial rewards. Grand, in contrast, does not. He lacks almost all sense of commercial survival. Holed up in his room, he pours over volumes of philology. Ironically, Rieux remarks, just such insignificant people often escape plague. Once more, as a point of reference, Camus' earlier fictional character of Meursault won't ask for a transfer; neither does Grand ask for salary raises or advancements. To both men, their leisure time is of prime importance. For Meursault, that time is spent swimming, going to the movies, and making love. Grand struggles over perfecting the beginning of a manuscript. Both men are, strictly speaking, nobodies—statistics, figuratively; actually, counters of statistics.

This inconsequentiality, however—isn't this, in a broad sense, definitive of Oran? In spite of their greed and thrift, there are no millionaires in the city, there are no artists of repute, no statesmen or politicians—there is actually no one known outside the city walls.

Rieux considers: none of these people matter, yet such a major tragedy as plague—what possible reason could there be for its singling out Oran? What logic, he wonders, is behind the destruction of Oran? Rieux has proven himself to be a man of logic; this pondering is quite in character. And, at this point, Rieux has pronounced the word "plague," but has not wholly adjusted to its revolting reality. He is still in vague, unbelieving awe, as if the word had barely left his open mouth.

Before leaving this chapter, there are two more incidents of credit for the doctor. Exhausted and preoccupied by the fever patients, he agrees to drop by and discuss a matter with Cottard concerning something about which Cottard is irritatingly vague. Originally, the doctor had suggested that Cottard drop by during consulting hours, but clearing his head of plague thoughts, he sympathically responds to the fellow.

The doctor gives Grand credit for being a man of feelings. Is it, however, Grand who has admirable feelings toward his fellow men or is it Rieux? One should question, at this point, whether Rieux is wholly to be trusted. Making decisions about motivation and not succumbing to the evaluation of the central figure's is one of the hurdles in learning to read literature. Rieux says that Grand "confessess" to dearly loving his nephews and sisters. He even admits that his heart responds whenever he recalls his deceased parents. Rieux's observation of Grand has Oran as relief, a town which becomes uneasy at the suggestion of affection. As yet, Grand has to show us any real sympathy. Even with Rieux, on their way to the laboratory, he suddenly dashes away to spend the evening with his bookish project. Grand's character takes on ambiguous shapes.

Before Oran is finally quarantined, Dr. Rieux confronts one more tangle in the local snarl of red tape. The Prefect, or local magistrate, must be dealt with. His stand concerning the seriousness of the plague is important because he is the self-deceiver, one of the safest—and most despicable —of roles. The Prefect sounds like a Liberal, but is an arch Conservative; he imagines himself encompassing each of his city's crises with sage wisdom and acting accordingly. But when he says that prompt action should be taken but "don't attract attention," he is pitifully similar to the civil rights fighter who supports protest marches as long as they are done in good taste and don't "attract attention." The man is a coward, afraid of indiscreet remarks, and is actually very frightened of Rieux's charges of epidemic. But he is not alone. Another colleague of Rieux's loudly supports the Prefect's stand on the issue, explaining away the fever in vague, medical-book sounding generalities. Finally Rieux seems at a loss for an answer. Only old Dr. Castel says matter-of-factly that plague is their visitor. Rieux modifies his seeming indecision by saying that the symptoms are not "classic," and at this point his purist view is alarming. Is the man going to insist that definitions and clinical reports be compiled and printed? Camus is teasing our suspense. Rieux counters his introductory remarks by debunking them. He tosses semantics to the timid-tongued doctors. Word games are ridiculous now. Action is the only answer.

Irritated that Dr. Richard would sarcastically accuse him of having proven the disease to be plague, Rieux insists that he has *not* proven plague. He has simply *seen* something as deadly as plague with epidemic proportions. Rieux then insists that they must act "as if" it is plague. Only then can they perform responsibly and efficiently.

The final and short scene of the woman dripping with blood, stretching her arms in agony toward Rieux, is another incident to help us see Rieux as a man who is aware of human cries for help. He has fought throughout this chapter for official resolutions to help just such people. In the relaxingly furnished quarters of a municipal official, amid a background of professional-sounding doctors and their medical jargon, one is far from the bloody pus pockets of the city. Rieux is arguing from a distance, from scenes he witnessed on the city's outskirts, and here his opinions are so contrary to most of those assembled that he might seem absurdly radical in his insistence. He leaves the room of doctors, a room of health and sanitation and goes outside, into the fresh air — now full of disease, and he sees bloodied evidence that affirms his stand for us and stiffens his resolve for action.

In Chapter 8, the plague and municipal efforts play tick-tack-toe. The plague tallies a few more deaths, and officials respond with a brief notice or two in obscure corners of the paper and small signs at obscure city points. Officially, rats and fleas are to be exterminated; illnesses resembling the mysterious fever are to be reported and patients isolated. Cleanliness is to be observed. Perhaps, it is hoped, the plague will then take care of itself.

Cottard's character now takes on greater significance. Grand reports that a complete change has taken place in the man and Rieux does some firsthand observing. Camus delineates some of the manifestations of a guilty conscience, but does not yet answer all the why's of Cottard's behavior. The reader should imagine and reason possibilities for himself by asking such questions as: why did Cottard try to commit suicide? Why does anyone attempt suicide? Because of fear? Fear of the future? of the past? of being alone? Guilt? Why does Cottard have an irrational fear of the police? A fear that they will be "rough" with him? He is relieved, you remember, when Rieux says that he will protect him. Consider, too, the scene in which Cottard's suicide motive was discussed. He merely replied "a secret grief," and refused to look at the officer. He insists on being left in peace, yet now he effects a change. He is suddenly animated, amiable, and altogether not himself. He now eats in luxury restaurants and flourishes grand tips. His remarks about his new acquaintances being good witnesses and his unease in a gossip about a murder case — these suggest to Grand that he has something on his conscience. His uneasy glances over his shoulder and his question about patients being arrested concern Rieux. Who is this man? He has tried suicide and recovered. Now, when the plague is eroding the town's edges, he has a new surge of life. He is now concerned that he live, that the police do not arrest him, and that his rights be fully respected. The taste of death in the town has invigorated him. Camus has swollen Cottard into major proportions in this last chapter of Part I; later the man will merit even more consideration.

Rieux admits that he is afraid. His hopes for a natural cessation of the plague are of course futile. The emergency measures are insufficient. Castel says that, ironically, something as tiny as fleas are at the root of the problem.

And outside nature is serenely blue, brilliantly golden. Spring's heavy perfume is in extreme contrast to the heavy smell of death.

Tarrou continues to observe, the old man spits on the cats, Grand writes, Cottard goes his way, the Spaniard counts his peas. Nature seems indifferent to the mushrooming fungus of destruction. Even the population seem indifferent as they perform their habitual, meaningless gestures. The death figure drops, then spurts up sharply. At last word comes from the head of officialdom — Rieux's efforts to convince the proper authority that an epidemic has begun are rewarded — the town is to be severed, totally isolated. Plague is proclaimed.

PART TWO

Throughout Part I, there is a sense of urgency and frustration. Death darkens the pages and we are among the few to realize what is happening as the toll increases. The frustration, however, is not wholly a life and death matter. Now, besides lives, there are values which are being annihilated. But Camus is structuring an irony. Death does not finally seem as important as knowledge does. We do not feel horror when the plague is proclaimed; the horror of the disease has already saturated us. We have read of its ugly symptoms — the heaps of rats' bodies and the blood- and pus-swollen sores. The plague is already very real to us. When the designation is officially announced the news seems good, for it means that although death, for awhile, is the victor, at least ignorance has been defeated. We read of the acknowledgment of the plague with a sense of relief. Truth has a victory. A lucid evaluation of the crisis has been achieved, the enemy has been revealed and can now be confronted.

Part II re-begins the chronicle in a different tone and with a different sense of time. The tone is less intense. Remembering the first days after the gates were closed, Rieux pulls back the focus of his narrative for a long general view. Here and there he recalls events that link disjointedly to one another — hands scribbling last notes, the look in lost eyes, feet wandering aimlessly. This is how it was, he seems to be saying and his tone is that of a man who has survived, but only barely. As a participant, he is almost absent; he is the raconteur and he speaks of a new element of time. Previously, in many lives, there was never a definite yesterday, a definite tomorrow and today; they were all part of an ambiguous dimension. Now the plague has shut the city gates, walled out the outside, and given a name to the hours prior to closing: that time is Before. The present, the now, is particularly frightening because it is seen against and as a part of a sequence of days and nights of living and dying. At least, then, the future had always been there—somewhere—even if it hadn't been seriously considered. Now even its existence seems in doubt.

Because this first chapter of Part II is a jumble of summary, perhaps it is best to begin considering Oran's new environment and the adjustment of the townspeople toward it. Like children thrust into a dark room, they are taken by surprise and caught unprepared; perhaps "dark room" isn't an exaggerated analogy: this new environment of Oran is like a world turned upside down—by accident, loved ones are away from the city, there are no letters, no telephone calls, no word from Out There. Several times Rieux refers to the city as a "prison house" and as a "lazar-house," and of their existence as one of exile.

As for adjusting—to face a problem does not necessarily mean that one faces it honestly. Few Oranians, it would appear, do. In general, there seem to be two ways of coping with the quarantine. At first some people succumb; others invent diversionary escapes.

Rieux describes those who give up as ones re-walking where memory has now made certain streets precious. He also speaks of those who enfold themselves in nostalgia; they create new habits, slow down their pace, and orient themselves toward waiting for the inevitable. Then there are those who do not give up, but who run. They run after hope. They hope letters can be sent someday, so they continue writing. They send telegrams, but realize that clichés and platitudes are the most concise and satisfactory texts for communication. Finally they realize the futility of any messages. The telephone arteries break down early. No amount of processing can handle the swollen flow. The next step is make-believe: waiting for the renewal of train services, the jingle of the phone, of the doorbell. Why this creativity? Largely because their pasts are full of remorse. Thus, they try changing; they ritually remember a mother's face throughout the day; they become model husbands for the wives beyond the walls. All these activities are their answers for ways of living under a sentence of death.

Of particular interest is how the plague binds men together and then, ironically, cuts them apart and rebinds each man within himself. Each man is as trapped as his neighbor; no one has special consideration under the plague's regime. There is an immediate leveling of social distinctions. All are equally in trouble, but they cannot comfort one another because they have never done so before. They have never expressed conventional emotions, and thus it is frustrating and useless to speak of the extreme emotions that the plague produces. The people talk past one another. They are doubly imprisoned — within Oran and within themselves — and this double-barred atmosphere of each man is awesomely new and menacing.

Besides the Oranians, there is one more type of prisoner in Oran. Rambert is such a man. He is a journalist, trapped here without a loved one and outside his home. Rieux pities him most. But we should remember that the plague is unrespecting.

Lastly, Rieux suggests that the Oranians are lucky — a strange statement. But it has its genesis in Camus' fondness for irony. The Oranians are lucky because their suffering is selfishly and limitedly personal. Because no one feels great compassion, they escape the deepest distress; Rieux mentions indifference being taken for composure. His irony is icy when he concludes that this limited despair saves Oran from total panic.

Finishing the random rememberings of Chapter 9, Rieux now concentrates on a subject dear to the people of Oran — their commerce. And only by considering what must certainly have been one of their gravest trials can we arrive at more of the truth about those days.

The plague has sealed the harbor. Money has stopped flowing in and out of the bay, and once again there is irony as Rieux describes several Oranians gazing out at the corpse-like ships afloat. The Oranians, you remember, seldom looked at the bay or responded to the natural sea beauty on their city's edge. Now they look upon a scene of stagnation. Commerce has ceased. In comparison, people seem of lesser consequence. Perhaps this enormous natural symbol of death, more than most any other factor, staggers them. They cast about, worried and irritated, for someone to blame.

To blame the Prefect, their business leader, seems natural enough. The city's business has failed, the city's chief is to blame. They seem like children blaming their mother because rain has begun to fall. The control of gasoline and foodstuffs confuses them; their failure, however, to understand the death statistics is plausible. Before, they thought principally of themselves and of their accumulation of money and material things. Death held little interest for them — particularly when it was a numerical statistic. Now comparisons are futile. Imagination, as an antidote, is impossible because the city's supply has long since atrophied. And so most of them either run from realizing what the plague involves or give up.

Who is making money? Only someone or something able to furnish hope or illusion for the troubled: bars and movie houses. Alcohol and the silverscreen are instant relief for personal misery that is festering. Pathetically, movie house crowds do not diminish when it becomes necessary to begin showing re-runs. Nor does common sense seem to care when taverns boast that spirits are the most effective agents against infection. For some, then, there is money to be made from misfortune but, for most, commerce is indeed dead. With expected irony, Rieux remarks that the idle crowds filling the streets make the city look festive and holiday-like.

For the remainder of Chapter 10, Rieux leaves his commentary to record three conversations: one with Cottard, one with Grand, and one with Rambert, the journalist. To each of the men he is a kind of father-confessor figure.

The brief Cottard episode is disturbing. In the midst of death and confusion he is still the beaming fellow that we left pages ago. His behavior is totally incongruous. His anxiously happy questioning about the plague's getting worse, his jokes about grocers getting rich – these seem almost the actions of a madman. He could be easily tagged a psychotic if he didn't mutter that "We'll all be nuts before long." He has come back to life in the poisoned air of Oran, but what's more important – he seems to realize why he is now happy and why he must seem ludicrous and "nuts."

Why does he talk to Rieux? There are two possible reasons: first, Rieux has doctored him, shown kindness, and offered to *protect* him; second, Rieux is a doctor and can function meaningfully only when people are sick or dying. For the first time in months Cottard finds himself functioning, if not meaningfully, at least satisfactorily – and in the shadow of a plague. The values of the men are antithetical, yet Cottard is reaching for fraternity. Dr. Rieux is admirable; the plague increases his chances for stature. And because Cottard has a new sense of well-being, he resorts to a superficial analogy to provide himself with some kind of peer. Yet there are moments when he (and we) can see another analogy. If he is happy because he is surrounded by people waiting for death sentences, perhaps it is because he has his own sentence waiting for him – a legal one. His earlier fear of the police supports such a supposition. For the present we know very little about Cottard, but should be aware of his increasing uniqueness. Camus intends for this character to carry considerable symbolic weight.

Cottard meets Rieux in the morning, two days after the gates have been closed. The same afternoon Grand comes to Rieux's office and, stimulated by a picture of Rieux's wife, becomes suddenly talkative about his past.

In this scene Grand's character loses much of its previous vagueness. His mulling over of the past is exactly what some other Oranians are doing, but Rieux has said that those who suffer remorse have turned into escapists. This is not true of Grand. He has remorse, but considers and weighs the liabilities of his past actions. His wasn't a glamorous or even a happy marriage — which shouldn't surprise us, knowing Grand even as superficially as we do.

He was a shy young fellow and felt protective toward Jeanne. They shared, one day, the loveliness of a Christmas-decorated shop window and were married soon afterward. Knowing Camus' affection for natural beauty, and having Oran's commercialism as a background for Grand and Jeanne, we might wonder if their sharing of happiness — for what seems to be the first and last time — in a shop window, artificially contrived to be beautiful in order to induce people to buy, isn't a comment on the meagerness of their chances for a full, rich life together. Grand's tone is fatalistic as he continues the episode.

His wife's leaving was admirable. Here was revolt. Because her life with Grand was bleak, silent, and doomed did not mean that she had to submit to its certain fate. She did not even have a lover who promised her happiness. Her remark that one needn't be happy to make another start suggests that groundless optimism is as ridiculous as the pessimism that her marriage was fostering. The important thing is the fresh start, the refusal to be trapped by convention or environment. Man has a right to change. This is Christian and also existential. Marriage had become a habit for Jeanne and Grand; its banality became unbearable. The only honest courage was to rebel against the morés of Oran that urged acceptance of a barren marriage as inevitable and final — even good because it had been decided and contracted. A decision, in an existential sense, is never irrevocable. There is always scope for insight, growth, and change.

Grand continues that he has always wanted to write and justify himself, but he sees his failure to find the words as a flaw in his will power and in his vocabulary. Could he justify himself? His attempt to write the perfect book is cerebral, a kind of passionless fantasy. Too often, his frustrated love of words seems to be a grotesque parody of his indifferent marriage.

With both Cottard and Grand, Rieux does very little communicating. Just as Oran is sealed off, so these people seem to be fenced apart. Cottard needs Rieux for support — someone solid whom he can trust, to whom he can mutter a weakness, and as someone whom he can bounce wisecracks off. Their talk is over in minutes. Grand's contact with Rieux is a bit more fruitful. He confesses for the first time the circumstances and the consequences of his failed marriage. There may be a degree of self-deception in his narrative, but his attempt to ponder is admirable. It is, in a sense, as fresh a start as Jeanne made years ago. And Grand's story has its effect on Rieux. For days the plague has been foremost in his mind; now he sends his wife a telegram expressing his concern and hope for her recovery.

Rambert's talk with Rieux takes place approximately three weeks later than the meetings with Cottard and Grand, and it is longer than the talk with either of those. Rambert insists on being an exception, on being released from the fate imposed on the Oranians. He wants Rieux to give him a certificate of release. Rieux notes that the journalist talks "incessantly, as if his nerves were out of hand." This is significant because Grand and Cottard also talked in this fevered tempo.

There is another similarity among the three men. Within the core of each of their conversations is a secret. For Cottard, his secret is a crime; for Grand, it is his miscarried marriage. Rambert's secret is that he has discovered that love and happiness are all he really cares for. Now, as though he is asking for a parole to go back to Paris, he appeals to Rieux. The plague has stopped him in Oran and caused him to realize that he is failing to love his wife as completely as he might. As the two men talk, Rieux picks up a small boy who has tumbled down. Ironically, he cannot right matters quite so easily for Rambert. Rieux says that Rambert has an excellent subject to write about in Oran. This sounds callous and ironical, and there is probably a vein of irony here, but there is deeper truth. The future for everyone in Oran is uncertain. Today, even tomorrow, may be one's last. To escape is impossible. To plead is futile. Rambert is a journalist and, however valid and heartbreaking his discovery that he has a potential for human warmth and love, nothing can alter the black-bordered present. To write about the plague is quite a worthwhile task; in fact, for Rambert this seems his only rational course of action. He has talent and training for reporting and here is a subject for him. To try to right an unsatisfactory past is impossible for all three men. The present, as Rieux tells Rambert, is their only time. For Cottard, this means a perilous freedom and a brotherhood with the threatened populace. Grand seems to be *thinking*, if not about the plague, then at least about the past, and thinking is an Oranian rarity. Rambert has, admittedly, a larger problem. He is caught within a strange city, the probable victim of a hostile and indifferent disease. He is totally alone and must now put all of his values to test if he is to survive with his integrity intact.

After he leaves Rambert, Dr. Rieux considers the journalist's slur that medicine has hardened him and that he deals only in abstractions. Rambert's remarks stem, of course, from his disappointment and failure to get a certificate of release, but there is a certain truth in his attack. Death and sickness are both concepts and realities; Rieux deals with them in both senses. In addition, Rieux's professional pace is extremely taxing: long hours of diagnosing, of treating, and of disposing of the dead. Often one must, in such an emergency, become as abstractly enduring and as effective as one's enemy. Couple this with the temperament that originally creates a doctor and the result is an anomaly. Rieux's heart is, no doubt, more sensitive than any in Oran, yet a doctor cannot survive on onion-skin sensitivity the way a poet can. He must keep emotion alive — in spite of habitually seeing sickness and in spite of daily seeing death. Death can easily become the norm, sensitivity an outmoded burden. More than anyone else in Oran, Dr. Rieux has continued his declaration of war on death and on the plague. He honestly admits to occasional periods during which pity dies and he becomes indifferent, but it is during these times that he sleeps and forgets and heals an exhausted mind and body.

He ends the chapter with an incident which is a kind of travesty the plague has produced. Doctors must physically battle members of a family in order to remove and isolate the plague's victims. The once welcome face of a doctor is now as foreboding as though he were wearing a mask of death. Here is one more type of isolation within Oran. Already we have seen the city isolated, then large numbers of citizens isolated by selfishness and ignorance; now we have the isolation of the sick. This concept of separation is increasingly walling in the city and its prisoners.

Chapter 11 is brief but highly dramatic and most important. It concerns the role of the Church during the plague — what its attitude was and how it battled Oran's murderous enemy. More than any single scene thus far, this chapter is loud and vivid and, as a reader, you should not overlook Camus' art in readying us for its drama. In the novel, as in any other art form — music, painting, poetry — rhythm is necessary; the tempo and the modulation of mood must be in balance before an artist is satisfied. The result is beauty, but unobtrusive beauty — a whole so skillfully produced that one is usually unaware of the separate parts and their tension. A critical analysis seems the proper place to call attention to some of the mechanics of esthetic pleasure in literature.

Consider the whole of Part I. Frustration fuses the individual scenes and builds steadily until the last sentence is read with the same intensity that one feels at the culmination of a Chopin crescendo. After this emotional exercise one is not ready for an immediate, feverish movement. It is necessary now to have a breather—to relax before the next burst of theatrics. Camus gives us opportunity to do exactly this. After Part I he begins an unhurried reminiscence through Chapter 9, concentrates his recollections upon commercialism in Chapter 10, and finishes the chapter with three conversational scenes, each a little longer than the last and each more important in the quality of personal revelation. Camus moves from the general to the less general and then to various lengths of specifics before presenting again a full chapter of action.

For Chapter 11 there is special preparation because there is more than a confrontation between major characters. Camus presents Religion versus Plague. Of course the character of Father Paneloux is significant, but the Church takes precedence. Since man's beginning, he has worshiped and feared some aspect of the natural world and has hoped in terms of an Eternal. Faith in a Something larger than man has milleniums of tradition; Camus' ideas challenge all these years of seemingly instinctive faith. In this chronicle, alongside the Oranians, the Church is on trial. It is, however, not the cave of safety that critics often accuse it of being. It does not ignore Oran's epidemic. But neither does it attack it forthrightly; instead, the Church injects reason into the plague's power. Before the Week of Prayer's Sunday sermon, people had been harried by something irrational and meaningless. This is no longer true. The Church has defined: the plague has a beginning and, ostensibly, an end. It has originated in the sin of Oran, its purpose is punishment, and its termination is dependent upon repentance. The logic of religious truth is responsible for this interpretation.

Objective narrative is probably impossible when recording what Rieux (and Camus) would consider ignorant, if holy, sermon-shouting. One should be aware that this chapter is not as objective as Rieux has said his chronicle would be; there is irony shot throughout its length. In the first sentence, Rieux means that the word *truth* be understood conversely. Truth is impossible for the Church. Truth comes only after unbiased thought, repeated analyses, and admitted mistakes. The Church, never erring, once again applies its subjective, cover-all formula of "sin = punishment" to this current crisis. There is further irony in Father Paneloux's being an expert in deciphering ancient inscriptions. Deciphering hieroglyphics may be possible for the priest, but deciphering the meaning of the plague is beyond his capabilities. There is additional irony in the chapter's imagery. The church service occurs during a torrential downpour and when Rieux uses such words as the "swelling tide of prayers," the "backwash" of invocation, the "overflow" of the congregation, he is building, tongue-in-cheek, image support for a major irony. Here, in the cathedral, away from the rain and the plague, people have gathered for a rebirth of hope. But do they receive hope?

Before the congregation enters the church, they undergo a baptism of soaking rain. Then they enter, and Rieux notes the smell of their soggy, wet clothes; this suggests the soggy, wet rats of Chapter 1 which escaped from Oran's sewers to die in the streets. Now, in a reversal, the Oranians are soggily leaving the streets and going inside a church to escape the plague. They come for help and for blessing, but find themselves intimidated, brow-beaten, and charged with criminal acts; they receive spiritual death, a parallel to the death of the rats. The sermon will not rouse the populace to coping effectively with the physical menace which is slaughtering them. The sermon prescribes soul-flailing and prayer, but not practical precautions. It compounds confusion by creating guilt and fear when strength and courage are needed.

Finally, there is another example of irony. The long sermon is highly effective because it is so passionately powered with emotion. It descends with the fury of the rain outside. In fact, the pounding of the rain and the pounding of Paneloux's rhetoric join forces to drive the crowd to its knees. Yet, when Paneloux has captured their wills by emotional means, he exhorts them to "take thought." Of course what Paneloux actually means by "taking thought" and what Camus would mean are two different concepts. Paneloux desires the congregation to take *his* thoughts. Thought, for Camus, would include thinking, not a substitution of mass confusion or mass acceptance of a doctrine of punishment handed down by a furious representative of the Unknown.

Besides the idea of "taking thought," there are two more ideas concluding Paneloux's sermon which Camus would champion, but which he would interpret antithetically. The priest charges the Oranians with "criminal indifference." Camus, in his novels and essays, pleads for an end to indifference among men. Paneloux refers to man's neglecting God; Camus' concept is in terms of a conscious and intense humanism.

Paneloux concludes his sermon saying that a prayer of love might help matters. But after the orator has been so striking in his sermon about devils and bloodied spears, this suggestion is colorless and vague — a kind of post thought, a p.s. of love to soothe before he releases the congregation. Practical brotherly love and love's responsibility are ideas which we have seen in use — by Dr. Rieux. For him, and for Camus, these ideas of love and responsibility are primary and basic, certainly not vague and benedictional.

Before leaving the chapter, one might note that for a holy man, Paneloux's image during the service has an ironic blend of the satanic. He is described as looking massive and enormously black. His big hands grasp the pulpit; the connotation is exact. Grasp is exactly what he does to the congregation that fills his church. He seizes their minds and grips until they are united in their shame. In addition, he addresses the public as his brethren, yet he indicts them in the second person, in the "you." He does not say that "we" — if he is a brother to his brethren — have deserved the plague; he steps outside his judgment.

If there is distinction in creating a national image, Father Paneloux is responsible for a share. Rieux noted earlier that the Oranians had felt a vague sense of union because they were equally in trouble. After the Sunday sermon they increasingly see themselves as criminals — prisoners serving sentences in the prison of Oran.

In addition, after the Sunday sermon, Oran begins noticeably to change; Rieux says that panic flares up. And, in part, Paneloux is also responsible for that, but he is certainly not the only factor to consider. To blame one man would be unjust and erroneous. The priest is probably more at fault for what he failed to do than for what he actually effected. Paneloux's responsibility lies in fanning the flames of panic — of giving impassioned and unverified reasons for the deaths. To his church service came people who were directionless and questioning. He hurled to them biblical horror tales of punishment by plague, convincing them that they deserved what was happening. He cried that the Oranians were enemies of God, were proud and indifferent — charges which are necessary ingredients for regular Sunday scourging; Paneloux had only to fire these charges vocally and imagistically until he saw heightened fear and awe in their faces. It was likely terrifying, yet what takes shape within people during a harrowing Sunday sermon has partially dissolved even by Monday morning.

At the root of Oran's panic is probably the resurgence of fresh deaths. Death has vivid bloody traces; it is visual. A sharp rise in its slaughter will stir panic before preaching will. But the combination can be lethal — especially if, in Paneloux's case, the preaching is fortified with reasons that are emotional fuses. Reasons, per se, without emotional fuses, are seldom as terrifying to people as a phenomenon which seems monstrously superhuman and destructive. Reasons can be weighed by examining their validity, considering who gives the reasons, what the man's background is, and how objective he is. Rationality usually averts panic. But alarming inquisitions — emotionally colored, misunderstood, and ignorantly interpreted — can be chaotic to a people panicking in the terror of a disaster.

For an example of Oran's growing panic, Rieux tells an incident that centers upon Grand and shows us what is probably one of the less spectacular of panicky reactions. By using Grand — the petty official ("the kind of man who always escapes" plagues and wars) — as an emotional measure, our imagination can begin with him and extend up the scale of Oran's panic. Rieux therefore does not have to be encyclopedic.

Grand trembles violently, gulps his drinks, mutters, and is on edge. He is short with Rieux, who doesn't understand the writing project or the weeks spent on one word. It is not known what Rieux thinks about Grand's problem with conjunctions, but within the circumference of this special trouble is, in miniature, a parallel to his problem in living responsibly. Grand has confined himself so totally in his off hours to his room and to the numerous revisions of the first sentence of his book that he has lost real zest for living and for reality. He seems to lack a social conjunction just as he lacks the proper *and, but,* or *then.*

Grand has, besides general troubles with conjunctions, an additional problem which he explains in detail to Rieux. He has evolved a scale of difficulty in choosing conjunctions. It is hard, for example, for him to choose between *but* and *and.* He doesn't say why, but it is important to speculate about. *And* is a simple joiner, whereas *but* can imply a stand on an issue. *And* joins two ideas innocuously; *but,* however, follows a statement, qualifying it with a second statement. One cannot utter a *but* impersonally; a new dimension of the speaker is apparent. And there is even an added risk when one uses a *but. And*'s can be pedestrian; *but*'s, though, register objection, and with different motivation, can even excuse the first assertion. One has to choose then between an unassuming *and* and a more forceful *but* and, if the latter, there is the additional burden of dilemma. For a man as introspective as Grand, here in his prose problems are exactly the kinds of decisions that, in a social situation, try his courage.

And and *but* are hard to choose between, but harder yet are *but* and *then.* Remembering what has already been said of *but,* think now about *then.* The word connotes a continuance, an evolution. It has a positive, growing quality. Grand's hardest choice, however, is whether or not to use a conjunction at all. To initially commit oneself is, simply, the most difficult trial.

With Grand, Rieux is sympathetic, but no doubt the genuine tenor of his feelings is partly supported by professional poise. He listens to the constant whistling of the wind and it conjures an image of Paneloux's holy flailing, slashing the air over Oran. Rieux's mind wanders as he listens to

Grand. The assertion that he made to Rambert—that he must face actual facts—finds a humorous echo in this chapter. He thinks Grand's dream of creating the perfect prose to which publishers will say, dramatically, "Hats off!" is largely impossible on account of the fact that publishers don't wear hats in the office. This bit of faraway musing that is stimulated by Grand's repetitive gesture of "Hats off!" is one of the few touches of humor in the book.

As for imagery in Chapter 12, you might note that Grand's labored first sentence is blessed with beautiful adjectives. This is in extreme contrast to his poverty and to the plague. The morning is fine, the month is May, the rider is a lady and elegant, her horse handsome, and their path flowering and running through a park filled with greenery. The words try, in addition, to jog with the horses' trotting pace. The sentence is stuffed with superlatives and promises. And ideals. The effort Grand has set for himself needs the will to join the first sentence with the second and so on. But Grand remains with his first words. Perfection: this is his dream. He must produce a perfect work to be left behind for posterity. This will be his life's labor and, even though it may seem impossible to us, at least he has not compromised. To some, he has wasted hours and pages of paper, but he has kept a dream alive. As beset with difficulties as he is, he has worked to produce nothing less than the best. There is nothing of genius in Grand, but because he is a human being, we should see that he does possess something admirable. Absurd, perhaps, but also admirable. Even within this nobody, this drudge, there is life and an individual sense of purpose being kept alive.

Rieux makes the transition from Chapter 12 to 13 rather cleverly. While listening to Grand talk about perfecting his prose, Rieux hears a commotion outside, goes to the window and sees people racing through the streets toward the city gates. He rushes down the stairs and pauses a moment. Here is evidence of the latest gossip—the epidemic of attempted escapes. Rieux literally dashes down the stairs into Chapter 13, pausing only a moment to ponder these escapes before beginning the subject of the chapter: the escape tactics of Raymond Rambert.

On first reading, this chapter seems only one more tale of frustration, but it is more; it is one part of a principal irony Rieux is preparing. Chapters 13 and 17 will be contrasted against each other. The former recounts the numerous business-like dead ends that Rambert encounters as he tries legally to leave Oran. Chapter 17 concerns his illegal attempts. Both systems —Oran's civic structure and Oran's underground—are ironically built of similar bureaucratic labyrinths and both refuse Rambert's request with the same kinds of Kafkaesque ambiguities. In addition, Rambert's attempts to

escape have a rather interesting quality of setting within this larger dimension of irony; Camus gives them a sporting image. Rambert is not the often-
seen, lean journalistic type. He is a squat, powerfully built, former football
player, and his refusal to accept the status quo of official and unofficial *no*'s
has the kind of muscular resolution that he has surely experienced on the
playing field.

Within Camus' situation of Rambert's ineffectiveness in his dealings
with the city and its underground, there are smaller ironies. For example,
the one official piece of paper that seems to promise most toward an official
escape is finally revealed to be only a form that all strangers in Oran are
requested to fill in. It has nothing of hope in it; it is information necessary
for Oranian clerks should Rambert die during the plague. Its purpose deals
with death, not life. The form has one function: locating his next of kin and,
probably most important, determining who will pay funeral and burial costs.
Living, we realize, requires many formal-looking forms, numbers, and com-
putations, but under the new regime of plague, death demands as thorough
an accounting of its citizens. There is only one word to describe such
irony: absurd.

Rambert has one small reason for hoping: he *is* being considered. With
everything else so topsy-turvy, he is not completely anonymous in this
strange city of the dying. His name is on paper; he is calling attention to
himself. Unlike so many of the townspeople, he has not given up. He is
demanding recognition through perseverance. And while reading of Rambert's perseverance, remember that Rieux is telling the story and that his
definition of perseverance is not the same as Rambert's. Rambert believes
that perseverance can finally, literally, pay off. Rieux does not. He is a
believer in perseverance, but only in this way: victory is an impossibility
when one struggles almost hourly with death as Rieux does, but perseverance gains in value when one realizes it must inevitably fail — that in the
darkness of an eternal nothing, it is all meaningless. To say a lifetime of *no*
to death and an ever *yes* to life, with unflagging perseverance, is the essence
of the revolt of Dr. Rieux. Rambert has not yet developed a philosophy concerning his perseverance; his present concept is little more than a sustained,
physical endurance. Currently he is in active protest and this chapter details its intensity — for example, his satiric but accurate catalog of the guar-
dians of the blind alleys he confronts: the sticklers, the consolers, the
triflers, etc. It is a sharp focus on the ineffectiveness of his hope and perseverance versus the absurd.

Some of the chapter's other ironies are these:

There seem to be two ways of "killing time" in Oran. One way occurred earlier – an enormous spurt of energy, panic, and hope of escape. Then, when this energy was depleted, it was replaced by a lethargic drift, and hope of escape has been replaced by a hope of the plague's waning. Thus, one can kill time during a death sentence by two diametrically defined ways of hoping. There is even a kind of absurdity in the phrase "killing time." Time is killing the Oranians while they imagine that they are "killing" it.

Rieux talks again of vast nostalgia, but in this chapter uses Rambert as a particular instance. Remembering his wife, Paris, and evening walks, Rambert visits the railway station. Here you should be aware of the parallels between his faith and that of the religious townspeople. Their faith is in God's mysterious justice; Rambert's faith is in his own determination and a justice based on rational logic. He does not belong in Oran and once this error has been corrected and processed, he will be released. Only for the present is he trapped. And, in the way that churches for the faithful are places of promise, so the railway station becomes almost a holy shrine, a station of deliverance, to Rambert. Former freedom takes on a sense of the hallowed. Like the cathedral, the station affords relief from the searing midday sun of Oran. Inside, both the cathedral and the railway station are dark and cool and made of stone. Rambert studies the timetables and departures posters as though they were religious stations of the cross. The defunct iron stove is fired only by memory now; its function is ornamental during the plague's duration. But for Rambert it is as evocative as a holy statue.

Before leaving the chapter, note the poetic images Rieux records. He refers to natural beauty in the midst of Oran's dying world. The satin-white marble tops of the cafe tables have a touch of Tiffany against the pearl-colored sunset. The immensity of this beauty seems indifferent to Oran, the exiled abscess on the sea, and the universe seems at odds with civilized notions of beauty. It makes the death of the day seem flawlessly beautiful; death in Oran is torturous, ugly, and foul-smelling.

Tarrou's notebooks are once again inserted to buttress Rieux's narrative. And because there is the sense of a philosopher behind them, the sketches remain convincing. His montage of quick impressions has the same mood that Rieux sustains – that of the ironic and the objectively aloof. Mounted patrols gun down cats and dogs. Tarrou doesn't comment, yet the implication is there. These animals may be carriers of infection, but they are also pets, symbols of home. As actual homes and family living are being exterminated by something abstract, human beings are destroying abstract symbols of that home.

The newspapers reporting the death statistics change their policy. They decide to publish daily totals. Why? The figure, although high, is not as staggering as the weekly total. You should remember that this is a reversal in policy. Originally totals were published weekly to keep the plague from having pressing daily existence. Now, of course, more factors have to be weighed and, in the public's interest, the less alarming the figure, the better. You should also note that in this atmosphere of death, a birth has occurred: *The Plague Chronicle* is born, publishing speculations, tips, morale boosters, and sure-cure advertisements. The townspeople rashly turn this parasitic publication into the city's most profitable enterprise.

The closed shops Tarrou speaks of are parallels of the dead in Oran, commercial corpses. And besides the dead, he speaks of the living, especially of their habits—such as the old man waiting for the cats—the habits such people retain lest they lose their sanity. He speaks also of those who actually crack within, open their windows and scream against the sky.

Again we read of the old Spaniard counting his peas, imagining that he has accomplished a twentieth-century feat by abolishing clocks from his house. He explains that every fifteen panfuls of peas is his feeding time. He doesn't need ridiculous clocks. In bed, however, for a quarter of a century, he is little more than a verbal mainspring of his timepiece of peas.

Rieux no doubt was sympathetic to Tarrou's ironic copy. Tarrou was sensitive to such incongruities as the plague's seeming to relax at dawn. Dawn, of course, is traditionally a time of hope and promise. The description of the sun as swollen connotes the image of the large swollen buboes which Rieux is many times daily called in to lance. At midday the town has a deserted look; the people are inside and seem like animals burrowing for shelter. Then, at night, the "hectic exaltation" exists, and although Tarrou omits the analogy, it is as if the people were drugged by the presence of a deadly vapor in the air.

Plague is no longer an irritant or even a frightening, shadowy menace. It is a fact and it has firmly rooted itself around Oran's perimeter. The suburbs have steadily felt its growth and have become part of a tightening belt of death that draws together toward the center of the city. Moreover, the disease is no longer merely "plague." It begins to have a diversity and an adaptability belonging to the philosophy of adapting and surviving. The plague seems human in its individuality, in its not being unchangingly classic and therefore combatable. This new variety of plague increases its successful destructiveness by threatening the townspeople with pulmonary innovations. Even the buboes begin to diverge from their initial appearance; now they swell and harden, refusing to burst.

Rieux's task becomes more difficult. In a parallel to his belief that men have individual value, he realizes that once again evil too has its individuality. Oran's enemy is not a textbook villain. It insists on being countered on its own terms, and because of the lack of doctors, Rieux must overtax an already overworked physical endurance. After his work there is little time for his own happiness. He cannot worry his mother, who has absolute faith that her son will always return home. He tells his mother that the day has been "as usual." To his mother, this means that all is well. But imagine what the word must encompass for him. *Usual* involves agonizing dying, shrieking relatives, and an ineffectual and insufficient serum. Rieux's anxiety about his wife intensifies his exhaustion. In an ironic similarity, the doctor's wife is as inoffensively comforting to her husband as he is to his mother. His wife writes that everything is going "as well as can be expected." Her phrasing is as ambiguous and as uncommunicative as the doctor's "as usual."

For the remainder of Chapter 15 Rieux is host to Tarrou and is more explicit concerning his driving, godless optimism. He identifies his mortal foe as creation and its natural processes. Rieux rebels against death, holding it at bay as long as possible, realizing that he will eventually suffer defeat. But for the doctor, a seduction of oneself with the myth of a life beyond death or a destruction of oneself through suicide or apathy can be only the acts of a coward. Death is the adversary of man. To ignore it or to succumb prematurely to it is unworthy of man. After all, man is alone in the universe; he knows of no other worlds nor of a divinity. He is his all and at the mercy of the universe's plagues — suffering, ignorance, and death. Man is his own savior and fashions his own values in terms of intelligence, persistent courage, and a belief in the absolute value of the human individual.

Rieux has not always had these attitudes. They have developed as he began to assert responsibility. Even his doctoring did not grow from a childhood aspiration. To Tarrou, he is rather offhand when he says that he wandered into the profession much as he might have any other. Later, however, he reveals what is probably closer to the truth. Rieux was a workman's son and the medical profession was the most rigorous challenge available. It is easy to imagine a man who now pits himself against the absurdities of the universe as once accepting the challenge that medicine offered. He also confesses to Tarrou the first time he took his profession seriously: when he first watched a patient die.

It is a burden to talk to Tarrou. Rieux is terribly exhausted to try and explain himself in terms of his own values and metaphysics. But he continues and Camus offers a natural image as a kind of stimulus. Rieux stares out the window and sees the vague line of the sea. Within, he senses a vague feeling of kinship with Tarrou and so he makes himself speak seriously with this fellow. In a later chapter, the sea will consecrate this friendship between the two men.

Tarrou, up to now, has been fairly nondescript, but instead of becoming more familiar as the book progresses, he becomes more notable. He offers to organize a civilian corps to act as plague fighters. No one else, besides the doctors, has taken such moral action. Tarrou is the first nonprofessional to commit himself and offer a plan for defense. His commitment is offered at a time when he and Rieux realize that soon the plague will be out of hand and that Oran's few doctors will be obsolete. Rieux recognizes the courage behind such a proposal but he questions Tarrou concerning the "consequence," which is of course probable death. In spite of Rieux's having seen excruciating suffering and dying, he is aware that good intentions have not always considered the grisly reality involved.

Rieux also asks Tarrou to come by next day for an injection before his "adventure." His chances are 1 to 3 for coming out of this undertaking alive. Rieux's motive for offering the advice is realistic and practical, yet his tone has an ironic quality. Tarrou counters with a story about a burial overseer, the sole survivor of a historical plague. He is being ironic in return and implying that life rarely has 1 to 3 logic. To communicate like this is to be seemingly ambiguous, but both men have learned now that the other is aware of man as a being alone in an indifferent world.

Although Tarrou's plan of action is exceptional, Rieux cannot describe its members in such language. It is a fallacy to ascribe heroism to men doing only what they must. Rieux sees Oran in these terms: in an emergency, people are tried and this means that they do what they must—help others and themselves to survive. There is nothing of the heroic in this. It is man's duty to himself and he recognizes this responsibility through clearsightedness. If, because of ignorance, he shirks, then ignorance is vice. Virtue is no more than fulfillment of a commonplace obligation. Real heroics are nonexistent. Neither does Rieux believe that callousness is the general rule. On the whole, he believes that men are more good than bad.

And, as a specific, Chapter 16 offers Grand. Because he is used to dealing with statistics, he is made secretary of the sanitary squads—certainly not a heroic role even though Rieux muses that if readers seek a "hero," Grand has such merit. This is not contradictory. Rieux's values are not those of the military; awards are not given to the foolhardy who fear nothing and accidentally survive an excess of bloody skirmishes. Grand's stature as a hero is equated with his capacity for commitment and the sustaining of that commitment. The heroic is the human.

Grand is thorough in his numerical analyses; he is even creative, taking great pains to plan graphs that will be as lucid as possible. He slacks at times, but he is a man; most of all you should realize this quality about him. He is a man and he is insignificant, has failed to give love, has remorse, has a ridiculous goal, but in this emergency, with quiet courage, he has offered himself and serves as best he can. He does not neglect his writing; through his close association with Rieux, he gains even a sense of humor concerning the precision he works with. Grand is, in his small but meaningful role, more human than the radio announcers who assuringly maintain that the world Out There suffers with Oran. Rieux sees Grand as having crossed a line of indifference and, even with only his little goodness of heart, as having adhered to the human condition. He has moved from the fringes of Oran's social structure into one of its major supports by becoming a part of a common solid unit combating a common enemy.

To review, Chapter 17 is a contrast to Chapter 13. The earlier chapter dealt with Rambert's futile but legal attempts to leave Oran; this chapter is a record of his vain trys to illegally escape. The nature of the underground, Rambert discovers, has all of the intricacies of Oran's official red tape, but his discovery costs him almost all of his hope for personal happiness in escape.

Rambert begins this round of disappointments by contacting Cottard, and by trusting in Cottard, Rambert exhibits a measure of his determination. It is as though he will grasp at straws to return to Paris. Cottard's revelation that he is a blackmailer and a criminal makes little difference to Rambert. But, for Cottard, during their conversation eagerness begins to build steadily. He is anxious for Rambert's friendship and his reason seems logical. Rambert is a journalist; after the plague Cottard will be arrested and he will need all of the character references possible. A journalist in debt to Cottard for his life can be a prime asset.

Rambert's repetition of failures begins with Cottard and moves through Garcia and to Raoul, Gonzales, Marcel, and Louis; with each man's promises Rambert's hopes are bolstered and subsequently burst. Then, between links of the chain of plotting, are days of silence and suspense. Rambert's nerves are worn by the continual tension of belief and uncertainty;

they are also frayed by the heat and the rising death toll. Often his surroundings seem surrealistic: deserted cafes, a rooster defecating on his table, conversation punctuated by a parrot's squawk and interrupted by queries from the dwarf waiter. Men, even with Rambert present, speak of him as though he were a profitable commodity. The city's lazy summer dogs are gone and the streets sizzle in the noon heat. All of the places of rendezvous have this mad, surrealistic atmosphere. At one time Rambert's collaborators insist on meeting in a hospital section of Oran, a section full of wailing relatives, clotted together in hopeful masses, crying for news from within. Another time, preparing the escape plans, the plotters meet near the war memorial — a spot commemorating those who did not escape death and their duty.

Rambert's change of mind to stay in Oran and assist Rieux and Tarrou is the climax of this chapter. The journalist has had to re-evaluate things of importance to him, and Camus is thorough in convincing us that the change, although Rambert continues to nurse a flicker of hope for escape, is genuine. At first the journalist was rational and insistent that he be allowed to leave the city. Failing, he became as rash and fierce as a Don Quixotish figure fighting the quarantine's decree. His goal was to return to the woman he loved. He was never afraid of the plague; as he tells Rieux, he has seen death as a soldier in the Spanish Civil War. Only now, because of the plague, has he honestly faced "what matters." His discovery that Rieux is also without his wife is no doubt the factor that finally transforms his determination to leave immediately into a resolution to stay and help Rieux and Tarrou. For chapters, there has been a dramatic irony in which Rambert has talked to Rieux and sighed for his beloved wife and Paris, then reined in his emotions and muttered to the doctor that he wouldn't understand. Rieux never tells Rambert about his own separation. Tarrou flings the facts in Rambert's face after Rambert has been particularly ugly and maudlin. As the chapter ends, Rambert has given up almost all hope for escape. He will stay until he can find a way of leaving, he says, but he is beginning to perceive that the present requires more serious allegiance and he does, almost totally, pledge himself to it.

There is also a more subtle factor, but one which is important in Rambert's decision. He has tried desperately to escape for one reason: to return to the girl he loves; yet all the while he has been so enmeshed in the escape he has scarcely thought of her. Self-deception, of course, can only be confessed by Rambert. Rieux is the narrator and he does not comment. If Rambert realized that his concern for personal happiness was for himself, he would be making no gross discovery. At heart, most people are primarily concerned with themselves. Theology has tainted this concern with labels of pride and selfishness, but in terms of Rieux's philosophy, there is room for understanding of this desire for human personal happiness. Rieux does not, of course, place his own happiness first, but he understands this desire. He also understands and accepts that he has a different instinct — a higher loyalty to all men in theory and to all men personally. He has accepted this burden of love.

The other important decision in this chapter is made by Paneloux; he agrees to help Rieux and Tarrou. By the end of Part II, then, all of the principal characters — Rieux, Tarrou, Rambert, Grand, and Paneloux — have joined to battle together as plague fighters. The plague has separated Oran from the outside and many of the Oranians from their loved ones, but it has begun to unite men of different temperaments and philosophies and to create a feeling of common humanity among them.

PART THREE

Part III consists of only one chapter — a short, intense chronicle of the crisis weeks in Oran, the time when two natural powers — the plague's rising fever and the midsummer sun — incinerate the city's prisoners. No longer is there active revolt. The panic-generated energy of Part II is gone. Despondency has stultified the population. As the chapter builds in intensity, corpses are piled quietly in ever-higher heaps, and Rieux does not dwell with the monotonous minutes of daily living, waiting, and enduring. His concern here, for the most part, is with the dead and dying, and because most of the section deals with the details of interment, Rieux has, like the Oranians in their task of withstanding the fever and the summer heat, his own test. The dying and the burying of which he must speak have loathsome particulars. Oran's crude mass burials would have tempted most writers to create the most vividly dramatic inferno imaginable, the volume's longest chapter. Rieux, however, controls his sensational subject, writes succinctly, and reports what he saw, not lapsing into melodrama. His sense of objective purpose concerning the chronicle has the same perseverance that he has demonstrated in his doctoring.

Rather than exaggerate, Rieux uses imaginative images and factual realism for the chapter's atmosphere. Once again he uses the words "prisoners" and "prison-house," reminding us of the image most common to Oranians. He describes the summer in provocative detail: the blistering, savage heat, heightened by the dirt storms, transforms the city into a gigantic bake oven, a larger version of the recently reopened crematory on the city's outskirts. One device, he implies, burns the living; the other, the dead.

All of the prisoners' senses are attacked in this chapter. The crematory assails the city with its stench; the skin is parched by drought, the eyes are stung by the dirt, and for weeks the wind shrilly whistles above the town, at times seeming to moan, at other times seeming to wail. Plague makes direct kills on some citizens; but on others it is more devious. The latter must battle on several fronts: fear, panic, and a feeling of exile and separation drain love from the heart; the senses are physically assaulted; the mind suffers major losses of hope and logic. Even imagination fails finally to recall separated loved ones, just as memory eventually succumbs. There is a trance-like adaptation to the plague. Horror reaches a point that fails to horrify any longer; it becomes a kind of monotonous norm, a habit. The Oranians live for the present, but are so despondent and spiritless that they cannot inject their living with meaning. Rieux insists that we not interpret this state as total resignation. There were some new habits to replace the old, and only a few citizens wholly gave up; the former steadfast refusal to be coerced by death is no longer in the city, but in its place is lethargy and a limboish state of waiting and enduring.

The changes within the people and within the city are important elements in this section. The plague, for example, is no longer concentrated in the outer districts. Suddenly it strikes the center of Oran, at its heart. Civil law is no longer effective and the city is under martial law. The acts which necessitate martial law are examples of highest absurdity, only a step below murderous anarchy. The burning of homes is not spontaneous, however. There are symptoms: mounted police gun down pets, symbols of home; first, the symbol is destroyed; later, the home itself. The action of this chronicle always builds; absurdities develop logically into one another toward the final culminating of atrocities in this chapter.

As always, there is irony. Homes are burned by people living on scraps of common sense. The plague proves to be so silent, elusive, and deadly that something has to be done. If serum is not always effective, perhaps germs are harboring in the safest of places — in homes. So homes are burned in moments of breakdown and irrationality. Martial law threatens the offenders, of course, but — with imprisonment. Within the prison of Oran, if a man burns his home, he is legally imprisoned and, once behind bars, certain of death, for nowhere is plague so thorough as it is in the prison-house. The irony increases when we realize that plague initially isolated Oran from the outside world. Then, once inside the city, after it had given the town if not a responsible solidarity, at least a united sense of common trouble, it viciously attacked *not* individuals, but *groups* (prisoners, nuns, monks, soldiers) and caused the members to be in individual quarantined isolation, miniature exiles of their city's exiled state. The chapter also records the separation of Oran into habitable and off-limit districts; the various kinds of separations will increase as the chapter continues.

When Rieux turns to the changes in burial processes, he remarks that his motive for retelling what may seem excessively repulsive is not morbidity. His tone here is defensive, but justifiably so. Especially to an American audience of amateur analysts, many of whom have never seen the systematic strokes of slaughterhouses, much less the chaotic extermination and the seemingly inhuman acts Rieux means to recount, the grossness of the chapter might seem too Gothic for belief. Since Rieux has said earlier that he has told only what happened, his artistic integrity cannot be questioned. Thus an audience of today might interpret his including these scenes as traceable to morbidity or to another neurotic genesis. Freudian divining has popularly replaced the horoscope in contemporary living; each system has labeled sections with precast futures, and Rieux (Camus) was aware that many readers might—even as early as twenty years after, in a comfortable well-civilized country—evaluate this chapter as the dreams of a morbid necrophiliac. Thus his word of caution reminds us that what we are reading is based on fact.

Note particularly in this chapter the circumstances of the burials. The civic authorities, once more, are identified with their endless paper work. Official forms, Rieux says, are the most important part of burials. A satiric attitude toward the men in charge is a convenient viewpoint and perhaps too easily superficial. Although the men seem to be strangling themselves in red tape, they are fighting the plague as efficiently, and often as humanely, as possible.

To forbid vigils is to suggest a lack of feeling, but isolation of corpses is a health precaution. In a similar way, speedy funerals appear to be the end product of a speed-oriented society, but the health factor is paramount. Propriety is the principle behind separate pits for men and women after cemetery plots are filled. Then, of course, when separate pits are impossible, Oran's officials conceive of stratified burial—alternating layers of corpses and quicklime—as the most competent alternative. Even the utilization of streetcars, at night, to transport the dead en masse to the crematory has humane efficiency as its motive. All of these absurd, unbelievable acts are part of a plan to struggle against Oran's enemy; they may seem barbaric, but the plague demands such survival tactics.

And then the worst is over. When the city can withstand no more, the plague begins to level off. Had it continued its killing, Rieux projects, carloads of bodies would have been dumped into the sea. It is interesting that in 1941, when Camus was jotting ideas for the novel in his notebooks, he had decided to have a sea full of corpses. Of course, he was more of a symbolist then. Several years later, he had lived through a world war and an occupation by enemy troops. His country had been witness to bestial atrocities; these he used in this book to serve his literary purpose more effectively than the elaboration of a literary symbol. Although he intends his chronicle as an allegory, he does not sacrifice realism on the primary level for blatant symbolism. To date, man has not resorted to mass sea burials. By 1947, however, open pit interment, filled by the blades of bulldozers, had occurred under Nazi supervision. Camus does not jeopardize his book's strength with exaggeration. His realism includes only acts actually committed by man.

PART FOUR

After recording the particulars of Oranian burials in a complete chapter, in fact in a complete section, Rieux now takes up the situation of those who were living during the period of lethargy. The first half of Chapter 19 describes more fully the drugged state of general despondency, and brings us up to date on the principal characters. It especially examines Dr. Rieux's responses to the exhausting spiritual and physical fatigue. The second half of the chapter is quite different. As a contrast, Cottard, from Tarrou's notebook sketches, is presented, still happy and smiling.

The lethargy refuses to lift itself from Oran. Even the October rains do not cleanse the town of its hold and the townspeople continue to exist for the moment at hand, but see their present without a context. Rieux uses, as an analogy, soldiers held under continual fire and strain. Both suffer similar stupors, he says. This lethargic state of mind lulls Grand into sentimentality; he talks of Jeanne more often and feels deeper remorse. Rambert continues to maintain some hope for escape. Tarrou loses the colorful diversity that was in his early notebooks. Now his subject is primarily Cottard. The narrator reveals several unexpected reactions of his own — unexpected because he is usually reticent about his personal life and unexpected because they are confessions of his feelings of loss. Rieux has so successfully convinced us of his physical and mental strength, neglecting his personal complaints, that he sometimes loses a sense of human individuality. Here he modifies the impression of a superhuman with devoted perseverance. He admits that the plague has fiercely exhausted him and that he has had to harden himself as a preventive against collapse. Under the strain of growing deaths and the increasing ineffectiveness of his serum, he feels less and less competent. At the same time, he questions whether or not in the face of this growing futility, his decision to send his wife to a far-away mountain sanitarium was wise. He is certain that he could have helped her make a good recovery.

This chapter re-humanizes Rieux; he feels a lump in his throat as he stares at the collapsed sleeping position of his colleague, Dr. Castel. Rieux even talks to Grand of his personal feelings, something he has never done before. He cannot say whether or not the plague is more fierce than it was yesterday; he can only measure his own competence, and the result is negative. Medical aid grows more meager. He can only diagnose; he cannot cure. Throughout the epidemic he has resisted death as thoroughly and as rapidly as he could save his patients. Now, however, his serum is losing its strength and his own physical vigor is wasting.

Ironically, Rieux concludes that because his strength is being sapped, so he is being saved from perhaps overwhelming sentiment and pity. Confrontation with such extreme disaster might strike down a man with alert senses and sentiment. Previously, at the beginning of Part II, he had noted that most of the Oranians were saved from disastrous panic because of their lack of pity. Now he remarks that he is saved from disastrous sentiment because of exhaustion.

Rieux clarifies another misfortune of the lethargic state — the slackening of Tarrou's medical crews. No longer do they take personal precautions of hygiene and vaccination; their sense of self-preservation is slipping away.

Obviously Cottard — criminal, black marketeer, and fugitive — is a dramatic contrast to this infectious weariness, and because of Cottard's uniqueness, Rieux includes a few of the sections of Tarrou's notebooks which center on this fellow. Cottard is rather patriarchal in his pity and affection for the townspeople. He has already suffered the fear of distrust and insecurity; the present despair of Oran makes him somewhat of an elder citizen. And, like an older member of the community, he most enjoys hobnobbing with the younger set, walking at night, joining the flow of the crowds into theaters and coffeehouses.

Yet one can be somewhat objectively sympathetic toward this human rarity. He most fears what many people do: solitude and the feeling of being an outsider. For the first time, he belongs; he has a niche in the human condition. He also has a clever logic rationalizing his own immunity. He theorizes that he cannot contract the plague because he carries his own death sentence and men never die of two illnesses. One infection immunizes a man from all other infections.

The concluding scene is, somehow, amusing—perhaps because it seems so apt. Nothing less than a highly ironic Creator, in this case Camus, would have trapped the opera company of *Orpheus* within Oran when the gates were sealed. The opera contains the identical elements that the citizens are experiencing. Orpheus' laments and Eurydice's vain appeals from Hell are ordinary, common Oranian acts. The theme of lovers separated is exact, current realism. It is little wonder that the opera is performed again and again, and is popular and successful during the season of plague. Even the actor portraying Orpheus catches the rhythms of his surroundings and improvises an extreme grotesqueness for his final position of defeat. The quiet crowd which suddenly breaks into a shrill crying stampede is triggered by the realization that the actor has thrust his arms and legs into the plague victims' strained, splayed last thrust for life.

The plague, for the present, offers life to Cottard. But to no one else has it been so instantly gratuitous. It has forced Grand to reconsider his entire past, particularly his lost marriage and the values of his present daily living; it has tested Dr. Rieux's belief and devotion to his job of keeping Oran alive and it has also revealed his human failings. Tarrou's plan of the civilian sanitary squads was conceived because of the plague's dramatic emergency. All these men have changed; unlike Cottard, each of them has sworn to maintain a personal revolt against the monstrous disease that threatens their city's entire population. But two characters have yet to be fully tested: Rambert and Paneloux. Both have enlisted as plague fighters, but Rambert's offer was not quite a wholehearted pledge and Paneloux's decision came from Christian duty, not from a love for man or from a crusading spirit of Good versus Evil; his faith is tried in a later chapter. Chapter 20 is crucial to Rambert's integrity.

Chronologically, Chapter 20 precedes most of 19; the latter, however, was used as an overall review of characters after the crisis, plus the notebook jottings about Cottard, and for a graphic look at one of Oran's centers of pleasure. The brief theater scene is crucial because unhappiness, sickness, and poverty are becoming Oran's daily tenor and Oranians are therefore seeking out the last bits of pleasure in the city.

Chapter 20 is not general like 19, nor does it deal with several different matters. Rambert is stage-center throughout. The chapter is structured in this way: Rambert contacts Gonzales and his agents, then discusses his leaving with Rieux. Afterward he meets the Spanish agents and, before leaving, returns to Rieux. Returning to Rieux, of course, is synonymous with his decision to stay in Oran until the plague is defeated and the gates are once more open.

Although Rambert still retains some hope of escape, there are hints in the chapter that foreshadow his decision to stay. Another two weeks of waiting grate deeper into his residue of hope, and his long hours on the sanitation squad fatigue him but make him aware of the value of work versus a life of idleness. He now talks little about his plans of escape; no longer does he boast. When his nerves at last shatter, he runs toward the sea crying to his wife and this release of emotion is his last genuine grasp for happiness. Afterward, he walks through the last phases of the plans for escape, but silently considering, listening to others and to himself.

It is not surprising that Rambert is caught off-guard by Rieux's telling him to hurry if he means to escape. Rieux is not an absolutist in his humanitarianism. Nor has he evolved a finished philosophy concerning his actions during the plague. He has acted and has listened to his heart and his conscience. Rationally he knows he could have escaped with his wife, supervised her convalescence, and claimed that he was only doing what was his by "right of happiness." But Rieux would not have been happy; happiness is of relative value. Thus he says to Rambert that the journalist would not be happy if he stayed, that he would be dishonest with himself and with Rieux. Rambert, it seems, expected a sermon from Rieux; he wanted urging. The decision, however, to be valuable has to be Rambert's own. Rieux, an atheist, tells Rambert to claim his happiness and as a counterpoint, the mother of the two Spanish boys, a devout Catholic, gives Rambert essentially the same advice. She too understands why he must return to his wife: the girl is pretty, Rambert is sensual; he does not believe in God, man must worship and believe in something—even if it is no more than a girl, himself, and their love.

Rieux was absolutely correct to juxtapose these two scenes. Usually the abyss separating believers and nonbelievers is thought to divide two views of man, totally incompatible with one another. Yet here both sides wish Rambert to be honest and to be happy. An educated atheist and an illiterate Catholic mother elect to stay in Oran, yet they understand Rambert's desire to leave and will not damn him for preferring personal happiness.

The image Rieux uses during the suspense of Rambert's decision-making is that of a caged animal—not a particularly original image, but excellent for his purpose. Rambert is caged because he has wanted desperately to leave, but has stayed, worked with the sanitation crews, and found a value in hard work and a satisfaction in becoming part of a whole bigger than himself combatting an impartial, impenetrable, deadly plague. He is trapped within high, sealed city walls and he has tested their strength; they seem as sturdy as the plague. His animal-like qualities include the importance of sex to him. He wishes to return to Paris to make love to his wife. Until now, he had never realized how much he enjoyed and needed love-making. Rambert is physically virile, animal-like, and powerfully built. His bare chest is described as glistening with sweat, like polished wood, as he paces. In Camus' novels, sex is never the fulcrum that it is in other contemporary fiction. Either it is matter of fact or else mentioned in passing. Rambert enjoys a sensual life and it is important to realize that Rieux understands this desire. It is a fallacy to see the doctor as a valiant, asexual knight in surgeon's clothing.

The final scene in the hospital has, besides Rambert's affirmation, several other matters of importance. Tarrou has caught Rieux's frustration. Both men begin to feel that their revolts are becoming obsolete. Tarrou says that the doctors are becoming accountants. Rieux remarked similarly when he talked of the evacuations and the burials in Chapter 19.

The hospital is described as being pale green inside and the light as being like that of an aquarium. Hospitals are usually places of rest where one recovers his strength. They are like the sea in the sense that it is therapy for Rieux to swim; soon he and Tarrou will renew their determination and perseverance while swimming together, in rhythm. The hospital Rieux remembers as being not promising, not restorative and not recreative, like the sea. Instead, it is like an aquarium, like an imprisoned sea where the patients are once again locked in. Here, behind barred windows, they are imprisoned within the hospital exactly as they are imprisoned within their city. They die in the stagnant hot air that is also held prisoner.

The talk about the car running out of rationed gas and Tarrou's speculation that they'll have to walk the next day is an obvious parallel to the professional situation of Rieux and Tarrou. Their serum supply and its effectiveness is "running out of gas." They'll have to walk, might fall behind, and perhaps perish in the heat and fever of Oran's desert.

After Rambert tells Rieux that he will stay, we probably learn more about Rieux than we do about Rambert. The doctor questions him, testing his sincerity, and says that nothing is worth the exchange of whomever one loves. But this is Rieux's mind talking and he confesses that he has contradicted his statement by his actions. He doesn't know why he sent his wife away. He simply acted. There seemed to be no choice and he says that he has not examined yet why he did it. Immediately thereafter he and Tarrou assign Rambert to the surveillance of one of the city's districts. There are to be no congratulations and toasts for Rambert's conversion. The plague is still rampant and must be continuously contested.

After the chapter describing the mass burials, Chapter 21 is probably next most successful in catching our sympathy for the plague victims. It is a chapter which gives us a full-length portrait of a dying child; it is also the record of Dr. Rieux's first witnessing of the entire last stages of the disease. Never before has he so minutely observed the tortured last hours before death. He is specific about his reactions. As he searches for the child's pulse, he feels an instinctive empathy attempting to pour his own strength into the boy; he aches to scream in protest against such vile injustice. His revolt against death and disease is a kind of madness, he says, but he insists on the child's innocence. We, like Dr. Rieux, have seen until now only glimpses of death and last moments — never the full process of death.

Camus could have, without seeming awkward, described a lengthy death scene long before this. Rieux, being the narrator-doctor, might likely have sat at a bedside and early initiated us to the cries and contortions of suffering. But he deferred this scene until the reason for presenting it was crucial. The reason for this particular vigil is much more genuine than the simple disposition of Rieux into a sickroom would have been. The scene is inserted when Rieux is losing his endurance; in addition it regroups — besides Rieux — Tarrou and Rambert, plus Grand, Dr. Castel, and Father Paneloux together as multiple witnesses (and sufferers) of the death throes of M. Othon's young child. We have the opportunity to know all of their reactions, which won't be first terrified impressions, but will come from hearts already seasoned to death and suffering.

All of these characters are called to Othon's home to watch a last-resort experiment of Dr. Castel's new serum on the boy. If the serum is not effective, it is possible that plague will prove to be the victor. After the boy dies, there is general blank depression, but there is also a bit of optimism. Castel is impressed by the serum's lengthening of the suffering period. There seems to be a strengthening of resistance even if it eventually fails. This effect, you should note, also lengthens the chapter for readers, making us more exactly imagine the swelling, the convulsions, and the incessant screaming.

The young boy, even though he is unsuccessful, wages his own small revolt aginst the plague. Castel's serum gives him additional strength to endlessly scream in protest against the invisible death that burns and bites into his flesh. He fights and dies in a classroom, a room where he should have come for growing and maturing. On the blackboard, like a Camus crest, is a half-obliterated equation. Equations add up; they equilibrate and are based on logic. Nothing in Rieux's moral code will admit an equation that calls for an innocent child to suffer. The utmost in abominable evil is exactly what he is witnessing: the suffering of a young innocent child — conclusive proof for him that the universe is irrational and indifferent to man. No divine equation is possible, and so the logic of equations is almost obliterated. Paneloux's sermon linking sin with punishment will later be partially obliterated by a new philosophy after he is witness to the innocent suffering of this child in a schoolroom. At present, the priest is visibly shaken by the ordeal; Rieux's anger disturbs him, and although he answers the doctors dogmatically, the boy's death will ferment within him and he will reconsider Rieux's angry assertion that because of the child's innocence they have been joined and bonded.

The motif of separation is once again used in this chapter. The boy's parents accept Rieux's diagnoses with quiet terror and acquiescence. The father is sent to an isolation camp; the mother and daughter are confined to the quarantine hospital. Plague continues to multiply separation and exile.

Paneloux, because of the extreme philosophy in his second sermon, is even touched by this quality of the exile. We should be aware of the nurture period for this change in the man. It was not long after his "sin = punishment" sermon that the priest became a diligent member of Tarrou's plague fighters. And once at work he no longer supervised quiet last rites. Punishment, if he could still call Oran's suffering by that name, was no longer an abstract threat: it was visual, disgusting, and a fact. Rieux is aware of the priest's outer composure as well as the fear that grows beneath the skin. Death threateningly crackles around him and the priest knows that inoculations are never foolproof. His faith in divine vengeance is worn thin by the time he witnesses the death of M. Othon's child. Because he is no longer comfortable with his ready-made store of threats, he begins to question the basis of his faith. He begins to construct sermons from his doubts. Like Grand's gradual evaluation of his marriage and his literary work, Paneloux's quest for honesty begins. It is more thorough and serious in its consequences, but as necessary and as difficult as Grand's.

Paneloux was not alone in questioning his faith. The townspeople are confused and Rieux notes the reduced audience for Paneloux's sermon to the men. His congregation had generally decided in favor of prophecies, numerology, and speculative charms. The church offered little understanding and hope for their plight. The people seem to need an external order that is reassuring. If the church becomes distasteful, they turn to nature's logic and to mathematical chances and schemes. They are persistent in seeking a logical answer to their torment and a logical end to its massacre. Irrationality is generally denied.

Since his work as a plague fighter, Paneloux no longer speaks particularly loudly or distinctly. His gentle voice now says "we" instead of "you"; he has joined the ranks of his community. He is no longer one of the crimson-robed elite; his clothes have been stained by Oran's bloody suffering and Paneloux has been humbled. He has realized that death is not a symbolic angry fist in the heavens and he reminds his audience of its tangible presence. The change in Paneloux, since his earlier sermon, is largely this: suffering does not necessarily imply punishment; it is for Christian good and offers a trial during which we must continue to believe in God's plan. The plague's image has changed from that of a whip to that of a teacher. Living has been easy; this phase is for rededication. Once Paneloux would have assured the congregation of the eternal happiness waiting as the wages of suffering. No longer. He cannot loudly preach such promises because he has become uncertain. He can only believe that God has a reason that is unfathomable but that there exists a holy logic that must be trusted. He asks for complete belief in God or else a complete denial of God, an All or Nothing proposition. Paneloux's acknowledging that God is testing man's faith is akin to Rieux's viewing the plague as a test of one's humanity and integrity. Neither man asks for resignation and both desire active acts of faith. Paneloux asks that his congregation pray for a completion of the divine will, and in the meantime to trust completely in God's plan for good. He brings to his sermon many examples of the Church's reactions to previous plagues. It is evident that he has done a great deal of thinking and considering before this assessment of Oran's catastrophe. Above all, the priest maintains that God must be loved. Man must not allow unfathomable suffering to lessen his passion for God. Man must approve of God's will and make it his own.

Tarrou approves of the extreme position which Paneloux has taken for himself. In the army he has seen priests faced with Paneloux's dilemma. There too either a priest approved of the gross agony of death he saw as a part of God's good or else he denied everything.

Paneloux's faith, however, tests itself even more severely. The pamphlet mentioned by the young deacon suggests that Paneloux is considering not only the plague's illness, but simple sickness itself. His logic is this: if man is ill, then that illness is a part of God's plan. Doctors, by issuing medicine and performing surgery interrupt God's processes, a heresy. Rieux, you should note, sees his work as an interruption also—not of God's plan, however, but of death's irrationality.

When Paneloux is stricken, he abides by his city's regulations and asks to be taken to the hospital, but in the early stages of his sickness, he refuses a doctor's help. Strangely, the symptoms are not ordinary. His throat is clotted with a choking substance; later he looks as if he has been thrashed. (By the flail of God that whips the air over Oran? By his own questioning faith?)

The ambiguousness of his death is best interpreted as the result of a conscious will at work. Paneloux has seen such a variety of undeserved dying that he affirms the rightness of such suffering by joining the victims in their role in God's plan.

After three dramatic chapters, Chapter 23 begins quietly on All Souls' Day, November 1. Winter has not yet arrived to hopefully freeze the plague germs. Autumn is mild; a cool breeze replaces the hot shrill whistling of summer and the light is no longer blinding. The fall sky is pale and golden. Beauty, after being charred by the summer, surrounds the city of pestilence. Again, the irony of natural beauty is played against natural ugliness and death. This is a fairly common irony, especially in this book, but here it is used as a transition into another incongruity. The mass conversion of Oranians to superstition has clothed them even on mild days in oil-cloth raincoats because two centuries previously doctors had recommended them. Imagine how the city must have looked from above with its absurdly shiny, rubberized, uniformed citizenry.

Even a greater incongruity, however, than the raincoat costumes in the plague city is the lack of men and women carrying flowers to the cemeteries. Remembrance of death is no longer a once-a-year day. Dying has assumed such major proportions that one can almost say that life seems the exception. Absurdity, irony, and incongruity are increasingly the constant atmosphere of the city. Even Cottard, Tarrou notes, begins to toss off ironic comments. And Rieux adds his own, remarking that the crematory was blazing as merrily as ever; the plague seems as efficient as a civil servant, he says.

Dr. Richard proves in this chapter that even an educated physician can become as absurd as the plague. As the disease achieves the quality of an efficiency expert, he is relieved at its leveling out on the progress charts. The number of deaths has less importance than the fact that no longer is the toll mounting. Just as the populace looked for logic in the Church, in horoscopes, and superstitions, Richard (and the townspeople, we may assume, had he been allowed to inform them) hopes that an equation can be assumed concerning the plague's progress. His relieved optimism and his new sense of happiness in the face of plague seems impossible. Certainly absurd, but true. Dr. Castel is uncertain. His serum is being lauded, but he has learned not to trust his enemy and maintains his defense and his revolt against the illogical visitor. Castel survives, but with efficient irony the plague disposes of Richard, the optimistic doctor. Then, curiously, it allows itself to be more exactly diagnosed into two definite forms: pulmonary and bubonic. The latter is disappearing, the former becoming more frequent.

Still summarizing, Rieux notes the profiteering based on, in addition to raincoats, food supplies. A change has taken place once more in the social levels of Oran. Previously the city has been indiscriminately attacked. Now the rich can afford the steep prices, the poor cannot. Despondency naturally begins to give way to envy and protests. Journalists, as Rieux has noted, continue to defraud the public of truth. Camus, during his career as a journalist under wartime conditions, had been no doubt witness to many incidents of journalistic Yes-writers. Because Rieux uses more of Tarrou's notebooks at this point, we can probably assume that the truth about Oran is probably impossible to ascertain if one were to consult its newspapers during the plague period.

The notebook passages concerning one of the isolation camps has an interesting twist. The stadium is used as an isolation camp because it is large enough to accommodate the many quarantined family members. But remember this: the Oranians think of themselves as prisoners, encased within their city; here, they are again imprisoned. There is a coil-like pattern to their prison image, much like the maze pattern of their streets. The stadium once served as an arena for athletic events. Now it is filled with people sparring for life. Death can deliver swift punches; it is a formidable opponent. Escape is impossible; armed sentries guard the exits. The suspense is somewhat like the stadium fever of old Rome.

Tarrou visits the stadium with Rambert and Gonzales, two former football players, and the contrasts between the past and the present are more evident because of the presence of these men. The primary difference is the present lack of activity. The men in the stadium now do nothing and they are silent. The shouting football activity is gone. Instead of a rowdy, spirited comradeship, there is a core of silent distrust; anyone may be carrying death within him. There is also a feeling of futility. They can hear the sounds of life beyond the walls and, like Rambert, they have devised so many plans for escape. Then, after defeat, they have realized that they have thought so continuously of escape that they have failed to think of the loved ones they hoped to rejoin.

Tarrou's inability to tell M. Othon of his boy's suffering is humanitarian, but all men in the stadium know of the suffering that the plague produces. Othon asks for the impossible and is surely aware of what he is asking for.

Tarrou pities him; Othon is a judge and should have a measure of objectivity, but he has proven to be as vulnerable as anyone else. Staring at the setting sun he seems resigned, lost, and asking for kind favors.

Winter approaches but the plague does not abate. The only improvement seems to be the clean shine of the cold air. Rieux notes this fresh quality at the beginning of Chapter 24 and remembers the old Spaniard remarking about its pleasant coolness. The night scene on the terrace, as Tarrou and Rieux relax, is another juxtaposition of a pleasant natural world in contrast with the town, sleeping and dying during the night.

Rieux's response to the evening is given more space here than the brief, ironic asides he has earlier slipped into his narrative. The slow-paced, relaxed style also contains fewer contrasts of opposites. There seems to be a longer time for looking and contemplation. The quiet night is indeed satisfying, but not absolutely so. Sky and sea meet grayly and stars are tarnished by the lighthouse's yellow gleam. Night is beautiful, yet flawed. The universe is not always blatantly superior; it too has its moods and imperfections.

On the terrace above the city, Rieux and Tarrou share what Robert Frost speaks of in his poem "Birches." There are times when it is not cowardly, but natural and necessary to want to swing high and away on birch branches, and

> "... get away from earth awhile
> And then come back to it and begin over."

This isn't the desire of a recluse but of a man who needs a time-out. The doctor has spent seven months in continual taut revolt and he is aware that his perseverance is fraying. His angry lash at Paneloux, the irritation of doubts about his wife's recovery—all these he diagnoses as danger signs. There seems even to be a more satisfying act performed by Rieux and Tarrou than merely "getting away." Tarrou calls it "taking an hour off for friendship." The time away is not spent alone; it is enjoyed with someone who shares one's own values and beliefs.

Also in this chapter is more necessary background information about Tarrou. So far, we know hardly anything. Rieux has not explained; he has allowed us to know only what he knew before this night. Thus far we know that Tarrou appeared in Oran, kept notebooks, did not try to escape, and volunteered to organize the civilian plague fighters. He has been as steadfast in his struggle to cure as Rieux has been.

The father Tarrou describes to Rieux had, in Tarrou's words, a peculiarity: although he seldom traveled, he knew the arrival and departure times for all trains that stopped in Paris; in addition, he knew the changes that must be made if one wanted to go as far, say, as Warsaw. Tarrou's mention of this side of the man's personality and later Rieux's speaking of it suggest that it was not altogether an oddity. Both Tarrou and Rieux believe in and defend the value of each human individual. The hobby of Tarrou's father, insignificant and seeming strange to others, is definitive. All people have a personal "something" that might seem ridiculous to anyone else, yet it is a kernel of their individuality. Some people believe that they keep a cleaner house than anyone else on the block, others can hold their liquor better, and still others believe that they can appreciate a musical performance more sensitively than anyone else in the audience. In that same audience may be a woman who knows that she is wearing the most expensive diamonds there. All people have a sense of pride in some facet of their individuality, which if confessed to would no doubt sound peculiar, but to Rieux, they are symbolic of the valuable intrinsic worth that comes with one's birth.

Tarrou's reaction to a court trial before he actually witnessed a session was much like the Oranians' thoughts of death — vague and abstract. Even Dr. Rieux, you should remember, although he had treated victims for several months, had not fully experienced the plague's death throes until he watched the process take place within Jacques Othon. Tarrou's sympathy for the defendant was very much like that which Camus felt for a boatload of prisoners he saw in the Algerian port in 1938. Both men were confounded by the knowledge that these unfortunates had committed crimes and yet both Tarrou and Camus refused to assent to the verdict of punishment by death. Camus described his feelings in an editorial, saying that endless imprisonment was tantamount to death; thus he was grieved and felt that somehow it was as unjust to damn human beings for the rest of their lives as it was to take their lives as payment for crimes committed.

The disgust which Tarrou conveys in recounting the trial proceedings — the euphemisms for beheading, the duty of condemnation expertly pronounced by his father in a matter-of-fact fashion — is found in greater detail in Camus' essays on justice and death penalties in *Resistance, Rebellion, and Death*. Both men had early experienced the conviction that one human being may not demand the life of another. Tarrou's realization that even idealistic social revolutions shoot down the old order hardened his resolve never to harm another human being. Now that we have his story, we can understand the genesis of his early remark that he wants only to find peace of mind; he is haunted by the idea that he might be party to a kind of murder if he actively commits himself. His kindness to Cottard, his saying that he gives people chances—these few verbal hints at last take on meaning. Camus, of course, was himself troubled with Tarrou's dilemma. If he supported the French underground to demolish, for instance, a troop train he would be aiding his defeated country in its struggle against the enemy. But troop trains are full of drafted soldiers following orders and taking no pleasure in war. May one kill individually innocent human beings, even during a war, with good conscience?

Because Tarrou aids Rieux, he is often confused with the doctor. His helping Rieux stems from the monumental emergency situation and from his friendship and respect for the doctor. But Rieux wages active revolt. Tarrou's revolt consists in not joining forces with the pestilence. As nearly as possible he attempts to remain innocent. Rieux, following his conscience, cannot; he must act regardless of accidental blunders. Tarrou is attempting a mortal sainthood. Rieux says that he is attempting to be only a man. Tarrou's answer that he is less ambitious is exactly what Rieux said to Paneloux, after the priest had said that his goal was man's salvation. They are a strange kind of trinity: Paneloux, Rieux, and Tarrou. One seeks salvation for man, one seeks a definition of man through action, the other quests for a godless sainthood for himself.

Winter fails to freeze the plague germs but not the city's walls. Chinks begin to appear, metaphorically. More cases of the pulmonary type of plague become easier to treat; patients become more cooperative. M. Othon, the judge, asks to be sent back to the quarantine camp. He, too, has ceased to feel alone in his sorrow and has assumed the civic burden of a plague fighter. Letters can now be clandestinely sent and received. The outside world seems closer in spite of the dreary Christmas season with its empty shop windows, its deserted streets, and the robot-like citizens.

Grand's surviving the plague's ravishes is much like a rebirth. Plague offered crucial questions that had to be answered. The clerk does have a potential for a life beyond the boundaries of statistics and graphs. A sense of humor, objectivity, and responsibility are all tested and proven during his illness. Before the plague he had been another man, but now he has begun a letter to Jeanne, has demanded that Rieux burn years of accumulated manuscript. He makes a fresh start with his sentence.

The other recoveries in Oran are, as Rieux says, against all the rules. But this is how the plague began—against all the rules. It had been ousted from civilized countries and had no reason for attacking Oran. Nor were its symptoms exactly that of other plagues. Part IV closes with the ambiguity of the rats' return, but the implications are clear: rats are able to live again in Oran. The plague has begun its retreat.

PART FIVE

Oran does not begin to jubilate immediately at the first signs of the plague's waning. Hope has become so slender that it cannot bear the weight of sudden happiness. It must be strengthened with caution and a degree of fear. In spite of the plague's diminishing, Chapter 26 is not a cheerful one. Nursing their own hopes, the Oranians ignore the deaths of the scores of new victims. The weekly statistics remain all-important, but only as they reflect a dropping off of the total number of deaths. To be among first victims or even to be struck down at the plague's peak is to gain sympathetic thoughts, yet now that freedom and victory seem forthcoming, death appears more outrageous.

The blue winter sky may be taken as a sign of promise. Of course, had the plague still been rampant, the same sky would have seemed to be healthily jeering. But currently Castel's serum begins to be effective and the universe seems suddenly acquiescent, not almighty and indifferent.

Rieux refers in this chapter to the number of wild escape attempts that occur. Here he is being sociologically accurate. Oran had certainly been prison-like and most escape attempts occur during the last weeks of the sentence; temptation increases until common sense is overpowered. Once again the communal life of the convents is restored and although this seems very much like new pockets of self-exile, it is evidence that men are able to once more live without breathing death onto one another. Man is free to once again effect his own exile if he wishes. The plague has given him a chance for examination of his values; he must now rebuild his future in terms of what he has learned.

Rieux's images continue to be consistent. Earlier he had referred to Oran as an "island of the damned." Now he says that the inhabitants are like a "shipload of survivors." Time, he implies, isolated them, surrounding them with endless days of terror; now they are setting out on this sea of time toward the future.

Returning to thoughts of Cottard, Rieux ponders the validity of Tarrou's notes on the black marketeer, wondering at their increasing subjectivity. But Rieux himself is guilty of occasional lapses. As the plague became more abominable, he revealed himself more fully and openly. Tarrou's diaries also contain passages concerning Rieux's mother, who reminds

Tarrou of his own. He does not say that the women were saints, yet they have many qualities that Tarrou associates with his pattern of sainthood. Both women were humble, simple, gentle, and kind. They had a "dimness," he says. Perhaps this dimness is because they withdrew. Rieux's mother stays inside, is devoted to her son, and does not overly concern herself with the deaths outside. Tarrou is unable to do this, but he seeks reasons and justifications for the beauty of such withdrawal because it contains no harm for others and he is terribly afraid of committing an act against another human being.

Cottard remains unique. Rieux says that he does not share the high spirits of the city; no longer does he feel an indefinite lease on life. Death, not life, is promised him as soon as the city gates are opened. As the Oranians begin to come out of their burrows, he retreats and stays in his room more frequently.

Tarrou's remark that a return to a "normal" life means new movies is not that of a cynic. It is realistic. New movies will only be one of the many commercial changes, but he has chosen movies because of their illusion. Once more people can share someone else's life for two hours; they can leave their unexciting evenings and live through colorful, musically sung romantic ups and downs, or live the vicarious adventures of a secret service agent, even live, for two hours, within the filmed world of a plague. Whatever illusions they pay for will cost everyone the same amount of coins and at a predetermined time the illusion will be over. Life is being returned to the people and once again they can afford a variety of silverscreen illusions. After all, the return to life after the gates are opened will have all the outer aspects of Before. Yet even this will be an illusion. On each heart, in varying degrees, will be scars of the plague and each Oranian will have somewhat of a new dimension as an individual.

The chapter ends with the disappearance of Cottard. Fleeing into the night, he no doubt knows that his running is futile. Tarrou's diary ends, Rieux tells us, with his sensing an end. His tiredness is not ordinary; plague has entered his body. Both men, Cottard and Tarrou, are sensitive to the symptoms.

Rieux, in Chapter 28, relaxes and, like the Oranians, shares the prospect of a fresh start and a reunion with his wife. Absurdities will continue however. Tarrou's illness, the headache and a raging thirst are warnings that he will not survive Oran's plague. Rieux has never before refused to isolate a patient, but he keeps Tarrou in his room. Why Tarrou dies before the book's end is speculative, but perhaps this breaking of rules is significant.

Perhaps also Tarrou has always been, as he said in Part IV, too much on the "victims' side." This death, like Paneloux's is unique. The priest's death showed no definite symptoms of plague. Tarrou's, on the other hand, has an extreme conjunction of both forms — the swollen buboes and the pulmonary attacks. Just as Tarrou had advocated living — in silent courageous struggle against a murderous mankind, so he struggled against the plague. Othon's son had twisted violently. Tarrou is unmoving; he fights with silent concentration. At the bedside, Rieux notes ironically that the night sounds seem remarkably like those of a plague-free city. He imagines seeing the last flinches of the plague burning the body before him. Tarrou may be the epidemic's last victim. Perhaps this too is unlikely, absurd, and as irrational as he knew life to be.

Rieux is again reminded of his impotence to hold off the mightiest ravages of death. He has survived the plague and the rigorous exertion it demanded, but he is no more than human; he is weak, saddened, and can continue only to fight absurdly. But if Tarrou's death has saddened him, it has also raised new resolve for the doctor to continue his stopgap measures against death. His defiance has fresh conviction. It is his fresh start.

Rieux reflects on his failure to fully give and respond to love and what he says is very much like what Grand confessed — that he never was sufficiently physical and verbal to Jeanne. Rieux's and his mother's lives are somewhat like that. And neither Rieux nor Tarrou was given an opportunity to share a deep continuing friendship with each other. Perhaps, however, during the plague the two men helped each other more freely, willingly, and with more sympathy than would have otherwise been possible. Both men were of ironic temperaments, personalities which do not lend easily to simple affection. Before the plague Rieux was busy and Tarrou was aloofly inspecting the city. It is doubtful that the friendship Rieux contemplates could have been effected. The death of Rieux's wife is joined to the suffering he undergoes following Tarrou's death. He is brief about it, as he was about the worst days of the plague. Excessive grief and real love seldom find adequate words.

The remaining chapters of Part V are much like listening to the recording of a radio commentator who was present at the reopening of the city. New and old faces flow in and out of the railway arteries and Rieux especially is observant of the reunited lovers. Throughout the chronicle he has commented on the townspeople's failure before the plague to attain a more varied, joyous, appreciative sense of life. Thus if one were to paraphrase a common fault, it would be easy to say that they failed to "appreciate the moment." Now, he sees lovers wishing to slow their new moments into slow motion so as to savor all of its thrill. Memories will no longer be static faces and tableaux. They will be of flesh and blood again. Minutes are too quick for them. The slow motion of swimming through time would be more satisfying as they rush toward one another.

Rambert is used as an example of the change wrought within the people of Oran. Once an outsider, a stranger, he has become part of this community and is aware that he can no longer be oblivious to consideration beyond himself.

Rieux also describes those who returned and found no one waiting. For them the plague will remain. Like the last victims, these people are lost and ignored in the bursting of cannons and reunited love. But for the majority of Oran, today is timeless. Tomorrow clocks will cut the day into pieces, but today is a day that will never again exist. Rieux rings Oran's numerous church bells for us, colors the sky gold and blue; fraternity catches fire as was never possible during the siege. The misery of even yesterday is diminished. Someday it will be partly denied, but for the present human love is violently rekindled.

Rieux, revealing his identity, explains that perhaps his greatest temptation in writing the chronicle was to make it a record of his personal struggle. He has tried, however, to show himself as only a part of a large, suffering community.

He ends his chronicle not on the ecstatic, crowded city of new lovers, but by finishing Cottard's curious history for us. The plague-reprieved criminal has gone mad amid the loud happiness outside his window, firing into the crowd, attempting to destroy the gaiety that means his doom. The dog he kills is curiously like himself. Both have survived by being kept in hiding. Cottard is carried out loudly protesting and is vocally reminiscent of a plague victim. His arms are pinioned and he screams convulsively.

Grand has written to Jeanne, something he could never have accomplished without the plague's baring the truth about himself. His humor, as he says that he has done away with his adjectives, is also good news. His subject and verb are unburdened and can move as freely as he now seems able to.

Choosing to close the book with the old Spaniard's philosophy gives assent, at least in part, to its wisdom. The asthma patient recognizes that plague is sometimes little more than life and that combatting it is of no more importance than combatting daily injustices. He prophesies that much will be forgotten and, of course, much will. Life is always more important than the past and its dead; memorials can be erected to clear one's forgetful conscience.

The celebration's firerockets are spectacularly awesome. Only yesterdays ago death was described by such adjectives. Then the sky was colored by crematory smoke and life was razed by fiery temperatures. Rieux has written his book as a reminder of just such incongruities as a warning that "normal" times are always subject to plague, that the bacillus of tyrants and war most easily infect and destroy a nation ignorant of symptoms and consequences.

CHARACTER ANALYSES

DR. BERNARD RIEUX

The narrator is about thirty-five years old. He is a highly respected surgeon, but Tarrou thinks that he might pass more easily for a Sicilian peasant. For example, Rieux's hands are not long and sensitively surgeon-like, but broad, deeply tanned, and hairy. Rieux is of moderate height and broad-shouldered; he has dark steady eyes, a big, well-modeled nose, and thick, tight-set lips. His black hair is clipped very close.

He belongs to a small group of people whom Tarrou calls "true healers." While there is still time for him to leave Oran and join his wife, he refuses. He remains in Oran to fight the plague with all his talent and strength. There is nothing heroic about his actions. He fights death and disease because he has been trained to and because he conceives of his life having value only when he is continuing to help others combat death and achieve health. There are only two evils for Rieux — death and man's ignorance of it.

About his personal relationships with his wife and mother, Rieux has misgivings. His love for mankind is consummated daily, yet to those for whom he is husband and son, he feels that he is probably inadequate. During the plague's last stages he regrets not giving more physical and vocal affection. Rieux's flaws, including his exhaustion and his tears when Tarrou dies, are necessary for a correct interpretation of his character. He says in the chronicle that he has told only what was experienced by all, that he has not made the book a highly personal confession. He does not separate himself or his duty from that of every man. Rieux tries to be definitely human — no more, no less.

FATHER PANELOUX

The priest interprets the sudden plague as just punishment for the sins of his congregation. He is vividly adamant during his sermon and further confuses an already puzzled, fearful populace. Later, after enrolling in the plague fighters' battalion, he has direct contact with day after day of poisoned, contorted victims. Death and plague are no longer easy abstracts. After witnessing the long, agonizing death of a child, Jacques Othon, he reassesses his faith and preaches another sermon. No longer does he speak of punishment. Suffering cannot be interpreted except in the sense that it is of absolute good and part of God's will. He demands that his congregation and that he, himself, love and approve of this unexplainable curse. Either this, or man must deny God completely. His death has strange symptoms, not at all plague-like. He seems to will his own death in order to join the ranks of the victims. Assenting to the plague, convinced that it is part of a divine good, he joins the dead.

JEAN TARROU

A wanderer who comes innocuously to Oran, he stays to help Rieux battle the plague and becomes its last victim. Deeply convinced that his lawyer-father was wrong to demand the death sentence for a criminal, and later disillusioned when his revolutionary party guns down former heads of state, Tarrou believes man is too frequently a party to murder. He rejects rationalizations that include frequent execution of men in the name of justice. To Tarrou, murder is the supreme evil in the world. He refuses to be a party to it and thus is rather aloof. In Oran, he keeps notebooks about ironic curiosities which he observes.

So serious about life, he is not middle-aged, but a stocky young fellow with a deeply furrowed face. Like Camus, he is a chain smoker and greatly enjoys swimming in the sea, also a pleasure of Rieux's. He and Rieux do not essentially change during the siege. Grand, Rambert, and Paneloux are all different men afterward. Tarrou, however, dies with a strangely smiling courage, still a strongly ironic man. He sought inner peace by becoming his own moral sentry so as not to bring harm to others. During the chronicle his goal was to become, although he was an atheist, a saint. He sought an innocence impossible to achieve, quite a different kind of impossible absurdity than Rieux sought. Rieux's struggle, which he realizes will be finally futile, is not impossible. He lives ever-sympathetic with men, always aware of his human duty to heal. Tarrou's search is highly personal, highly spiritual.

RAYMOND RAMBERT

The former football player, and at present a feature writer for a Paris newspaper, is in Oran on assignment when the city is quarantined. He first tries to leave the city by appealing to the civil authorities. Then when that fails, he offers money to several shady characters belonging to Oran's underground. None of the contacts, however, are able to arrange a successful escape. Rambert feels unjustly exiled in this legally proclaimed city of exile. He has few friends, no family — in fact, no reason to be included in the quarantine; he is certain that neither Jean Tarrou nor Dr. Rieux can understand his constant demand for release. The plague changes Rambert from a hack journalist into a responsible adult. Early in the book, he pleaded to leave so that he could return to his wife. Later he willingly elects to remain in Oran and assist Rieux rather than take flight to claim a solitary happiness for himself. He has joined his conscience in a moral commitment to an allegiance higher than himself.

JOSEPH GRAND

The civil servant is fifty-ish, tall, and bent. He leads a dreary, quiet life until the plague seals off Oran from the outside world. Until then, he spends his free time polishing the first sentence of a prose-perfect book he dreams of writing. Stacks of scribbled pages do not deter him. He persists in writing and listening to the sense and the sound of his sentence number one and continues to fail. He has already failed to make a respectable income and also to hold together a marriage with a woman whom he is now sure he loved deeply. But however odd and eccentric he seems, he is among the first to volunteer to help fight the plague that threatens Oran. He contracts the disease, but recovers. Rieux had remarked offhandedly earlier in the book that he is the insignificant type that often escapes such disasters. The chronicle does not prove this though. Grand survives, not escapes. In the emergency, he reacted instinctively, doing his meager best to defend his city, and during this period of trial he gained an insight into his writing project and into the reasons why his marriage failed.

ALLEGORY

Attempts to explain an allegorical work are, at best, rarely satisfactory. Allegorical interpretations are as elusive and as tenuous as their interpreters. One critic will charge that the work has been diced into irreparable ruins; another will dismiss the same essay as superficial and general. Camus recognized this difficulty and remarked that only broad outlines should be paralleled in allegorical comment. To attempt a thorough analysis would be to suggest that the work was not art but contrived artifice. It is in this spirit of generalities that *The Plague* has been considered.

Camus' chronicle had been conceived as early as 1939, but was not begun until after France was defeated and the Germans moved their occupation troops into the country. During these years Camus kept a series of notebooks and many of the jottings in the notebooks suggest the multitude of ideas that Camus considered before his book was finally completed. Nearly all these early *Plague* ideas reveal Camus' concern for a truthful realism and a rejection of sensationalism. They also indicate his continuing insistence that his book carry his metaphysical ideas of the absurd. Initially Camus was even wary of the word *plague*. Late in 1942, he cautions himself not to include the word in the title. He considers *The Prisoners*. Later and more frequently he mentions the prisoner idea and, especially, the theme of separation.

Several kinds of separation are apparent already in the first part. Within the plot line, many of the characters are separated from one another by their small-time greeds, their lack of human love, and their indifference. There is also the separation of the living and the dead as the plague progresses into Oran. The ill are put into isolation camps and are separated from relatives and family. Finally, and of philosophical interest, is the separation of nature and the Oranians. The setting is awesome and beautiful — on the sea. Throughout the sick-tainted days of the epidemic, nature is radiant. Man's plight seems nonexistent. Here is Camus' crux. Man wants and prays fervently to be important to some guiding force in the heavens — something larger than himself. Yet there is only beautiful, sun-warmed silence; there is only separation between man and his universe.

What supreme irony that man should be in such total isolation and long most for the impossible. The universe is indifferent to us, to our plagues of whatever magnitude. Nothing is certain but death. We are isolated. Alone. These are the truths which Camus believed about existence and which he hoped to parallel in Oran's situation, cut off from the outside world and imprisoned by the plague. And, in this extreme situation, he created characters who would be forced to think, reflect, and assume responsibility for living. Death is faced by many of the Oranians for the first time — and with all the horror of a plague. This confrontation with death is mandatory for experiencing the Absurd. The symbol of the plague can, of course, represent any hardship or disaster, but rationally facing our existence is probably one of the most extreme of metaphysical trials. One never fully experiences until he has gone through a struggle for self-understanding and, in *The*

Plague, the symptoms of the rats suggest the confusion one undergoes before this long struggle. The symptoms of distress – of this need to understand oneself and one's universe – can of course be ignored, but finally one does have to face himself honestly and endure a plague-like period of readjustment to the truths one must live with. Within existential philosophy this examination period is mandatory. It is actually a reassertion of Socrates' "the unexamined life is not worth living."

There seem, however, to be few positive or concrete symptoms of distress before man comes to terms with his existence in the universe. On the contrary, there seem to be only negatives and nothings to confirm this distressed feeling. One must reach rock bottom and begin questioning a faith that began long ago to cope with the revelation of the frauds of Santa Claus, of stork-delivered babies, and the perfection of, at least, one of our parents. Everyone finally seemed composed of a measure of hypocrisy, greed, and selfishness. People become, simply, human. And with honest consideration even the superhuman becomes suspectedly human. The universe is ever silent. Prayer seems much less than even 50-50 certain. God's whimsy confuses.

Awareness of a godless universe and a thorough re-evaluation of one's life and one's civilization is of prime importance within the existential context. Man's struggle to adjust to his new vision, his guilty relapse into easeful hope for eternal life, and his fleeting thoughts of suicide – all these will plague him until he will, with new insight, re-emerge to live with the absurd vision, with spiritual hope, or self-impose his own death.

The plague is also a useful symbol for all evil and suffering. The old Spaniard suggests that life is plague-like and Rieux seems to argue for this possibility of interpretation. Facing a plague's problems is no more than facing the problem of man's mortality. Camus' atheism may at first seem repugnant, but it is affirmative because it stresses each man's role as representative in its responsibility and commitment. Camus does not tempt man to endure suffering or evil for promised rewards in the hereafter. He denounces evil and offers human dignity to men who will end suffering through action, not through prayer. He offers man the awful burden of total freedom to determine the fate of mankind – with no recourse to an always, all-forgiving deity. God can too easily become last-minute insurance. His forgiveness entitles man to exist in the lifeless monotony of Oran, living life selfishly and indifferently until crisis time.

Leaving the metaphysical and turning to the concrete, remember that while he was writing *The Plague,* Camus was living in a homeland occupied by German conquerors. His country was imprisoned as completely as plague might seal off its borders. There was destruction, death, and suffering. The cruel violence of this was as unjust as the cruelty of a plague. And Camus' chronicle is a personal affirmation of the worth of human beings and life *despite* — despite being exiled in the universe, despite being ravaged by disease and tyrants. It is a belief in life's potential for multiple meaning and fullness.

This belief is especially remarkable because Camus realized that the world was not conscientiously reacting to the symptoms of war. France, particularly, has been criticized by historians for succumbing too easily to the Nazis and delivering their country into German hands. But France was not alone. These symptoms were known to all countries, and because Part I of Camus' book deals with symptoms of the plague and the reaction of the populace to them, we might now consider the symptoms that preluded World War II and some of the national reactions. Further, we might recount some of the major national deaths before the United States actively entered the fight against the Axis powers.

Aggression was first initiated by Japan in September, 1931, when she moved into Chinese Manchuria. The trouble spot was oceans away. The Chinese made appeal to the League of Nations, who appointed a committee to study the problem. The committee verbally condemned the aggression, but no active measures were taken to repel Japan. Her next move was a deeper penetration into northern China.

The actions taken against the enemy, then and in Camus' book, were on paper — compiling, counting, suggesting. To combat either a plague or a hungry aggressor, piles of study reports often amount to the same kind of ashcan effectiveness.

The Chinese Nationalist government recognized Japan's conquests, but the rebelistic Chinese Communists refused, demanding that the invaders be driven out. They finally kidnaped Nationalist leader Chiang Kai-shek and demanded immediate military action against the enemy. But the Chinese continued to retreat and in 1938 Japan openly proclaimed a New Order. Chiang Kai-shek's empire was to be annihilated and all Occidentals were to be removed so that a new and completely Oriental government might be established.

Here was solid proof of aggression that should be halted, but because Japan had not declared war, could another nation label her actions aggressive? The policy of look-see (the same as that of Dr. Richard, Dr. Rieux's opponent, in *The Plague*) was generally agreed to at this time.

Meanwhile, happenings in Europe were somewhat parallel. In 1936, Hitler had sufficiently mesmerized the German people into a growing Nazi war machine. His first move was to march into the Rhineland. After World War I, this area had been a kind of no-man's land. Originally it was to have been ruled by France; later decisions filled it with Allied occupation troops. It was to be strictly demilitarized. Hitler's invasion was in gross violation of the Treaty of Versailles. Further, it violated the Locarno treaty, which reaffirmed the zone as demilitarized and which France, Germany, and Belgium agreed not to invade. Any offender would be attacked by the other two signers.

Camus could be justifiably proud of his nation in this crisis. While the rest of the world looked on at the Rhineland, France mobilized 150,000 troops. She alone responded. Other nations thought it unwise to engage in militaristics; some feared the label of "warmonger"; others simply saw Germany as arming her borders, a rather natural thing for a country to want to do.

In 1936, Italy overran Ethiopia. France, Britain, and the United States seemed indifferent.

Meanwhile, Hitler continued his expansion. Austria was swallowed in March, 1938; a year later, Czechoslovakia was overwhelmed by the Nazis. In America people went to their jobs, hoping for the best. Enjoying relief from the earlier Depression, they were not anxious to face the horrors of war.

During this time President Roosevelt delivered his "quarantine speech," stating that peace was being jeopardized by a small portion of the world. Later in 1939 he speculated that "in case of war" the Germans and the Italians might win.

Even earlier than Roosevelt's quarantine speech, however, Winston Churchill (a Rieux or Castel figure) had the reason and the imagination to consider what confronted the world. "Do not suppose that this is the end," he said. "This is only the beginning of the reckoning...which will be proffered to us year by year unless, by a supreme recovery of moral health and martial vigor, we arise again and take our stand for freedom...."

United States armed soldiers came to Europe late. Only in December, 1941, when the Japanese attacked Pearl Harbor, did the United States officially enter the world conflict. Before this entry the Nazis had invaded Poland, conquered Denmark and Norway, defeated Holland and Belgium, driven through France, captured Paris, annexed Rumania, Bulgaria, and Hungary. Finally they threatened Britain with successive air raids. Then they turned toward the Soviet Union.

Throughout these years, the people of the United States had commented on these tragedies to each other over bowls of breakfast cereal. And, as the Nazi machine devoured the houses of European neighbors, the United States continued to go its way—like Grand, Cottard, Rambert, and many others of the Oranians. We hoped for the best, that this plague would sate itself and relent. Ironically, after we quarantined ourselves from the European conflict, we found ourselves in a kind of quarantine after Pearl Harbor. Our Allies lay wounded at the Nazis' heels and we were surrounded by enemies.

Thus not only can one see parallels in the French people's failure to curb German encroachment and occupation, but a general reluctance on the part of people everywhere to recognize the germination of the plague of war. Finally, of course, must come the formal declaration.

Even before their country was occupied by *la peste brune* (the brown plague), as the brown-uniformed Nazis were called, the French people did not consider the mobilization orders serious. Sisley Huddleston, in his book *France, the Tragic Years,* reports that the general comment was "It will be like last year." The people thought it silly to cry "Wolf!" when there was no real danger.

When war was official, there was the same sense of incredulity that Oran suffered. There was also death, but it was not caused by the kind of war fought in 1914. This time war was mechanized. Nazis parachuted their troops, had amphibious craft, and Panzer divisions. The French were ill-equipped and fear was as destructive as the Nazis' machines. This fear, plus the lack of any cohesion weakened the country. By degrees, waves of panic, dejection, and indifference swept the trapped people. At the war's beginning, even Camus was rather unbelieving; later he was morose when the conflict could not be averted. He blamed both the masses and the leaders for their weaknesses, just as in *The Plague,* he attacks the indifferent citizens and their wishy-washy officials.

The plague lasts almost a year; the Occupation of France lasted four years. During those years the majority of the French people clung instinctively to life, seeking out small pleasures, praying intermittently, hoping for signs but, largely, neither aiding nor resisting the enemy. The Resistance was not a large organization, just as Rieux's team was also not large. But they persevered, believing in the rightness of their efforts. It was not easy to murder men merely because they were Occupation troops. Tarrou's philosophy seemed most humane, but Camus and others finally took the stand that he writes of in his "Letters to a German Friend." Here he confesses the difficulty he had in affirming violence to counter the enemy. He stresses the agony that intelligence burdens one with, especially when one is fighting savage violence and aware of consequences of which the enemy is ignorant.

The despair and the separation were endured by the French people until the Allied troops liberated the country trapped behind the Occupational walls. And, like all men, like even those survivors of World War I, the French swore never again to let tragedies like this happen. Mankind, however, is free. Camus believes in the potential of the human race to avoid destroying itself. But he offers it the freedom to do so — under one condition: that each man assume his guilt for the holocaust.

REVIEW QUESTIONS

1. Considering only the remarks about Oran in Chapter 1, what can you say concerning the character of the anonymous narrator?

2. Rambert insists on leaving Oran; is it because he fears death? Why or why not?

3. What events prompt Tarrou to try to live as a saint? How does he define "sainthood"?

4. In general, what are the differences between the two sermons of Paneloux? What is responsible for the change?

5. Why does Rieux not consider himself a hero?

6. Why does Rieux say that Grand might be considered hero-like?

7. What is the function of Rieux's mother in the chronicle?

8. Account for Rieux's sympathy toward Cottard.

9. Of the many reunited Oranian lovers, why does Rieux single out Rambert as representative?

10. In terms of Rieux's objective narrative, do you think it necessary to describe so minutely the suffering of Jacques Othon? Why or why not?

11. What is accomplished by having Rieux and Tarrou take a night swim together?

12. What prompts Grand to ask Rieux to burn his years of accumulated manuscript?

13. Before he dies, does Tarrou find the peace of mind that he has said he seeks?

14. Does the book seem an obvious allegory? Why or why not?

SUGGESTED THEME TOPICS

1. Attitudes toward death in *The Plague*.

2. The advantages or disadvantages of an ironic tone (or irony) in *The Plague*.

3. Optimism and pessimism in *The Plague*.

4. Camus' ideas concerning religion in *The Plague*.

5. Imagery and symbolism in *The Plague*.

6. Happiness in Oran, before and after the plague.

7. A definition of humanism in terms of *The Plague*.

8. *The Plague:* an anti-Christian novel.

9. Characterization: successful or unsuccessful in *The Plague*.

10. Realism in *The Plague*.

SELECTED BIBLIOGRAPHY

WORKS BY ALBERT CAMUS

(In English Translation)

Fiction

The Stranger, trans. Stuart Gilbert. New York: Vintage Books, 1946.

The Plague, trans. Stuart Gilbert. New York: The Modern Library, 1948.

The Fall, trans. Justin O'Brien. New York: Vintage Books, 1956.

The Exile and the Kingdom, trans. Justin O'Brien. New York: Vintage Books, 1965.

Drama

Caligula and 3 Other Plays, trans. Stuart Gilbert. New York: Vintage Books, 1958.

The Possessed, trans. Justin O'Brien. New York: Vintage Books, 1964.

Essays

The Rebel, trans. Anthony Bower. New York: Vintage Books, 1956.

The Myth of Sisyphus and Other Essays, trans. Justin O'Brien. New York: Vintage Books, 1959.

Resistance, Rebellion and Death, trans. Justin O'Brien. New York: Alfred A. Knopf, 1960.

Notebooks 1935-42, trans. Philip Thody. New York: Alfred A. Knopf, 1963.

Notebooks 1942-51, trans. Justin O'Brien. New York: Alfred A. Knopf, 1965.

BOOKS ON CAMUS

Brée, Germaine. *Camus*. New Brunswick, New Jersey: Rutgers University Press, 1959. Revised Edition, 1961. A basic study of Camus' writings.

—— (ed.). *Camus: A Collection of Critical Essays*. Twentieth Century Views Series. Englewood Cliffs, New Jersey: Prentice-Hall, 1962. A valuable combination of reviews and critical articles written in the 1940's and 50's and scholarly estimates written after Camus' death.

Cruickshank, John. *Albert Camus and the Literature of Revolt:* New York and London: Oxford University Press, 1959. Camus' philosophical ideas are examined within the philosophical background of Kierkegaard, Nietzsche, Dostoievsky, and Jaspers.

Hanna, Thomas C. *The Thought and Art of Albert Camus*. Chicago: Henry Regnery, 1958. Analyses of Camus' essays, plays, and novels.

Maquet, Albert. *Albert Camus: The Invincible Summer,* trans. Herma Briffault. New York: George Braziller, 1958. A study of Camus' publications, delineating Camus' increasing concern with optimistic humanism.

Parker, Emmett. *Albert Camus, the Artist in the Arena*. Madison, Wisconsin: The University of Wisconsin Press, 1965. An extensive examination of Camus' journalistic essays, editorials, and articles from the 1930's until his death.

Thody, Philip. *Albert Camus: A Study of His Work*. London: Hamish Hamilton, 1957. An assessment and detailed interpretation of Camus' fiction and nonfiction.

NOTES

NOTES

NOTES

NOTES

NOTES